Old Testament Characters

BIBLE STUDY GUIDE

From the Bible-teaching ministry of

Charles R. Swindoll

INSIGHT FOR LIVING

Charles R. Swindoll is a graduate of Dallas Theological Seminary and has served in pastorates for more than twenty-three years, including churches in Texas, New England, and California. Since 1971 he has served as senior pastor of the First Evangelical Free Church of Fullerton, California. Chuck's radio program, "Insight for Living," began in 1979. In addition to his church and radio ministries, Chuck has authored twenty-one books and numerous booklets on a variety of subjects.

Based on the outlines of Chuck's sermons, the study guide text is coauthored by Ken Gire, Jr., a graduate of Texas Christian University and Dallas Theological Seminary. The Living Insights are written by Bill Butterworth, a graduate of Florida Bible College, Dallas Theological Seminary, and Florida Atlantic University. Ken Gire, Jr., is presently the director of the educational products department at Insight for Living, and Bill Butterworth is currently the director of counseling ministries.

Editor in Chief:	Cynthia Swindoll
Coauthor of Text:	Ken Gire, Jr.
Author of Living Insights:	Bill Butterworth
Editorial Assistant:	Julie Martin
Copy Manager:	Jac La Tour
Copy Assistant:	Delia Gomez
Director, Communications Division:	Carla Beck
Project Manager:	Nina Paris
Art Director:	Becky Englund
Production Artist:	Trisha Smith
Typographer:	Bob Haskins
Cover:	Painting by J. James Tissot, *Samson Pulls Down the Pillars*
Print Production Manager:	Deedee Snyder
Printer:	Frye and Smith

ISBN 0-8499-8288-X

Ordering Information

An album that contains twelve messages on six cassettes and corresponds to this study guide may be purchased through Insight for Living, Post Office Box 4444, Fullerton, California 92634. For ordering information and a current catalog, please write our office or call (714) 870-9161.

Canadian residents may obtain a catalog and ordering information through Insight for Living Ministries, Post Office Box 2510, Vancouver, British Columbia, Canada V6B 3W7, (604) 272-5811. Overseas residents should direct their correspondence to our Fullerton office.

If you wish to order by Visa or MasterCard, you are welcome to use our toll-free number, (800) 772-8888, Monday through Friday between the hours of 8:30 A.M. and 4:00 P.M., Pacific time. This number may be used anywhere in the continental United States excluding Alaska, California, and Hawaii. Orders from those areas can be made by calling our general office number, (714) 870-9161.

Table of Contents

Old Testament Characters

Scriptural character studies never fail to encourage us in our pilgrimage. That is one of the reasons God included snapshots of so many people in His Book. He wants us to see His truth reflected in all these lives—even in the most obscure and unfamiliar individuals.

The Old Testament biographical sketches are designed to help us identify with a few of the ancients. We'll smile and weep, frown and sigh, feel the stinging consequences of sin, and happily rejoice in the victories of various men and women. We will also see ourselves in a new light.

This is all part of the Lord's plan. Our faithful Heavenly Father has preserved each life in still portraits for our examination. I encourage you to study each one carefully with me. Stop, look, and listen for those insights that will open new doors of understanding. Don't be afraid to compare. God's Word is a timeless mirror that gives us a true reflection of what pleases Him and what grieves Him.

I am pleased to introduce each one of these people to you. As their lives are unveiled, my prayer is that you will receive helpful perspective and wisdom that will result in greater stability, a stronger commitment to biblical principles, and a broader awareness of how God works in our lives today.

Chuck Swindoll

Putting Truth into Action

Knowledge apart from application falls short of God's desire for His children. Knowledge must result in change and growth. Consequently, we have constructed this Bible study guide with these purposes in mind: (1) to stimulate discovery, (2) to increase understanding, and (3) to encourage application.

At the end of each lesson is a section called 🐢 **Living Insights.** There you'll be given assistance in further Bible study, thoughtful interaction, and personal appropriation. This is the place where the lesson is fitted with shoe leather for your walk through the varied experiences of life.

It's our hope that you'll discover numerous ways to use this tool. Some useful avenues we would suggest are personal meditation, joint discovery, and discussion with your spouse, family, work associates, friends, or neighbors. The study guide is also practical for church classes and, of course, as a study aid for the "Insight for Living" radio broadcast.

In order to derive the greatest benefit from this process, we suggest that you record your responses to the lessons in a notebook where writing space is plentiful. In view of the kinds of questions asked, your notebook may become a journal filled with your many discoveries and commitments. We anticipate that you will find yourself returning to it periodically for review and encouragement.

Ken Gire, Jr.
Coauthor of Text

Bill Butterworth
Author of Living Insights

Old Testament Characters

Samson: A He-Man with a She-Weakness
Judges 13–15

From Greek mythology to Saturday morning cartoons—from Hercules to the He-Man of the Universe—heroes loom immortal in our imagination. And no hero casts such a long and impressive shadow as Samson. His able-to-leap-tall-buildings-in-a-single-bound resumé reads like Superman's: killed a lion with his bare hands . . . slaughtered thirty Philistines who had plotted against him . . . defeated a thousand-man band of enemies with the jawbone of a donkey . . . destroyed the city gates at Gaza. But just as Superman was vulnerable to kryptonite, so Samson had a chink in his armor through which his greatness was sapped. He was king of the hill when it came to physical prowess, but when it came to women, he was a pawn of his own passions. At the core of his being, sensual desires raged hot. Samson's mother was a strong center of gravity in the home. But once Samson launched from there, he took off on a misguided orbit that revolved around three women—his bride, a harlot, and Delilah. His desires for these women formed a magnetic field that pulled him off God's course and put him onto a collision course that would eventually lead to his demise.

I. Samson and His Mother (Judges 13)

From a quiet, yet miraculous beginning to a tragic, yet triumphant climax, Samson's life encompasses all the elements of a Shakespearean drama. Act 1, scene 1 of Samson's life opens in Judges 13. As the curtain rises, a dark backdrop reveals sinful Israel in bondage to the neighboring country of Philistia.

> Now the sons of Israel again did evil in the sight of the Lord, so that the Lord gave them into the hands of the Philistines forty years. (v. 1)

Against this discouraging setting, a lamp of hope is lit for the nation. Lighting the wick is an angel of the Lord who visits the barren wife of Manoah:

> And there was a certain man of Zorah, of the family of the Danites, whose name was Manoah; and his wife was

1

barren and had borne no children. Then the angel of the Lord appeared to the woman, and said to her, "Behold now, you are barren and have borne no children, but you shall conceive and give birth to a son. Now therefore, be careful not to drink wine or strong drink, nor eat any unclean thing. For behold, you shall conceive and give birth to a son, and no razor shall come upon his head, for the boy shall be a Nazirite to God from the womb." (vv. 2–5a)

Hope's emerging flame begins dispelling the nation's darkness in the latter portion of verse 5: "and he shall begin to deliver Israel from the hands of the Philistines." In verses 6–7, the woman tells her husband about the divine encounter. Afterward, he entreats the Lord to have the messenger return (vv. 8–9a). Verses 9b–23 record that second angelic visitation. A godly, yet somewhat anxious father, Manoah questions the angel concerning the child's upbringing and professional future: "Now when your words come to pass, what shall be the boy's mode of life and his vocation?" (v. 12). Manoah is motivated not by *curiosity* but by *commitment*—a commitment to raise the child so he is best prepared for his destiny. This commitment is underscored by the parents' anxiousness to make a burnt offering to the Lord in reverential submission to His will (v. 19). In a miraculous display, fire shoots up from the altar toward heaven, and the angel of the Lord ascends out of sight (v. 20). Sometime later, a son is indeed born to this godly couple (v. 24). His mother gives him the name Samson.[1] Blessed by the Lord, the boy grows, and the Spirit of the Lord begins to stir in him in a mighty way (v. 25). And upon this scene the curtain falls.

Principle One

Sensuous children can be born of spiritual parents. A godly, biblical home life is no guarantee against sensuality, as Samson's life progressively illustrates. He was a child born of prayer . . . came as a direct result of an angelic appearance and announcement . . . raised by a family that was sensitive and obedient to the Lord . . . was blessed by the Lord . . . and was uniquely visited by the Holy Spirit. But take notes with indelible ink—if Samson's life teaches us anything as parents, it teaches us that even children with a spiritual head start can plunge headlong into carnality.

---

1. Samson is derived from the Hebrew word for "sun" and probably refers to "that which is distinguished, the pinnacle, one who is strong."

II. Samson and His Bride (Judges 14–15)

By the time the curtain rises in Judges 14, many years have passed. Samson is now a virile, young man whose hormones boil within him like pent-up steam in a pressure cooker. Unable or unwilling to control his passions, he sees a Philistine woman and becomes obsessed with her.

> Then Samson went down to Timnah and saw a woman in Timnah, one of the daughters of the Philistines. So he came back and told his father and mother, "I saw a woman in Timnah, one of the daughters of the Philistines; now therefore, get her for me as a wife." Then his father and his mother said to him, "Is there no woman among the daughters of your relatives, or among all our people, that you go to take a wife from the uncircumcised Philistines?" But Samson said to his father, "Get her for me, for she looks good to me." (vv. 1–3)

Samson's eyes spur his lust to break the dual reins of his parents' wishes (v. 3) and of the Mosaic Law (Deut. 7:1–3). Again, in verse 7, as if the Spirit is drawing our attention to the bent in his character, we are informed that "she looked good to Samson."

Principle Two

A sensuous person focuses on the external rather than on the internal. The first recorded words of Samson are, "I saw a woman." Three times in the passage Samson refers to the Philistine woman in exclusively visual terms. He does not mention her internal qualities. As attractively carved wood frames a Rembrandt, our external appearance should unobtrusively frame our internal qualities. When a frame is ornately carved, scrolled, and overlaid with gold leaf, it is easy for our focus to shift from the picture to the frame. And this is precisely why Peter warns: "Let not your adornment be merely external . . . but let it be the hidden person of the heart" (1 Pet. 3:3–4). When you look at someone, is your focus on the wood or on the Rembrandt? The appearance—or the heart (1 Sam. 16:7)?

In spite of this maverick's runaway lust, God is *still* in the saddle and *still* in control.

> However, his father and mother did not know that it was of the Lord, for He was seeking an occasion against the Philistines. Now at that time the Philistines were ruling over Israel. (v. 4)

Samson is to fulfill his destiny by delivering Israel from the Philistines—even in his disobedience. God worked through Samson's

3

lust to drive a wedge into the ranks of the Philistines—a wedge so strong that it would eventually cause the destruction of Israel's mighty foe. Verses 5–9 record an incident in Samson's life when "the Spirit of the Lord came upon him mightily" to help him overcome an attacking lion (v. 6). Later, a swarm of bees hived themselves away within the lion's carcass, out of which Samson scooped honey for himself. He uses this incident to pose a riddle to the thirty Philistine companions who had accompanied his bride to a seven-day feast. Bets are placed on both sides, and the riddle is put forth.

> "Out of the eater came something to eat,
> And out of the strong came something sweet." (v. 14)

The Philistines are given a time limit of seven days to unravel the riddle. By the fourth day, still stumped, they threaten Samson's bride into enticing him to reveal the answer to her. After days of pleading and weeping, she finally wheedles the answer out of him and promptly tells it to her countrymen. Just before the deadline, the Philistines answer Samson's riddle.

> So the men of the city said to him on the seventh day
> before the sun went down,
> "What is sweeter than honey?
> And what is stronger than a lion?" (v. 18a)

Realizing he has been duped, Samson's rage starts with a verbal accusation and ends with a violent act.

> And he said to them,
> "If you had not plowed with my heifer,
> You would not have found out my riddle."
> Then the Spirit of the Lord came upon him mightily, and
> he went down to Ashkelon and killed thirty of them and
> took their spoil, and gave the changes of clothes to those
> who told the riddle. And his anger burned, and he went
> up to his father's house. (vv. 18b–19)

Hardly in the honeymoon mood, Samson storms away to his father's house. Left behind, his wife is then given to one of his companions (v. 20). Sometime later, the harvest moon begins a tidal pull on Samson's libido. Before he knows it, he's at the door to his wife's room with flowers in hand. (Actually, it was a goat, but that doesn't translate too romantically into our culture.)

> But after a while, in the time of wheat harvest, it came
> about that Samson visited his wife with a young goat, and
> said, "I will go in to my wife in her room." (15:1a)

Enter the father-in-law to stand at his daughter's door, sandbagging passion's flood.

> But her father did not let him enter. And her father said,
> "I really thought that you hated her intensely; so I gave

her to your companion. Is not her younger sister more beautiful than she? Please let her be yours instead." (vv. 1b–2)

With thoughts turning quickly from romance to revenge, Samson's rage rushes to fill the suddenly vacated emotion.

Samson then said to them, "This time I shall be blameless in regard to the Philistines when I do them harm." And Samson went and caught three hundred foxes, and took torches, and turned the foxes tail to tail, and put one torch in the middle between two tails. When he had set fire to the torches, he released the foxes into the standing grain of the Philistines, thus burning up both the shocks and the standing grain, along with the vineyards and groves. (vv. 3–5)

One act of revenge begets another as the Philistines retaliate by burning Samson's wife and her father (v. 6). In turn, Samson strikes them ruthlessly with a great slaughter (vv. 7–8). Bound by ropes, Samson is given over to the Philistines by his fearful countrymen (vv. 11–13). Again, however, the Spirit of the Lord comes upon Samson, and he slays a thousand of his captors with the jawbone of a donkey (vv. 14–20).

Principle Three

The sensuous life brings one anxiety after another. The denial of Samson's physical gratification led to anger which, in turn, led to violence and then more violence. As Proverbs wisely observes: "A hot-tempered man abounds in transgression" (29:22b), and by that transgression a man is ensnared (v. 6a). The sensuous life is baited with enticing honey, but honey is *always* sticky, and the results of indulging in it can be tragic (7:23). Is the bait worth the heartache? Is the snare worth the sensuous step into transgression?

III. Samson and the Harlot (Judges 16:1–3)

For twenty years Samson ruled as judge over Israel (Judg. 15:20) and apparently ruled righteously and by faith (Heb. 11:32–34). However, we are told in Judges 16:1 that when he went to Gaza, he "saw a harlot there, and went in to her." Little did he realize that his walk on the wild side would lead him to a snare which almost cost him his life (vv. 2–3).

Sensuality may be dormant, but it is never dead. Like embers
smoldering beneath the surface of a thought-to-be extinguished
camp fire, lust, when fanned in the open air, can fuel a forest
fire. And invariably, someone always gets burned.

> For on account of a harlot one is reduced to a loaf
>   of bread,
> And an adulteress hunts for the precious life.
> Can a man take fire in his bosom,
> And his clothes not be burned?
> Or can a man walk on hot coals,
> And his feet not be scorched? (Prov. 6:26–28)

Samson's lustful escapades are graphic visual aids to James 1:14–15.

> But each one is tempted when he is carried away and
> enticed by his own lust. Then when lust has conceived,
> it gives birth to sin; and when sin is accomplished, it
> brings forth death.

Each snare in this tragic hero's life is tripped by his sensuality, and
like the bird that "hastens to the snare" (Prov. 7:23), it will ultimately
cost him his life.

Living Insights

Study One ━━━━━━━━━━━━━━━━━━━━━━━━━━━━━━━━━━━━━━

Samson is best known for his hair, his strength, and Delilah. We know
his hair was left uncut because he took the vow of a Nazirite. But what
was a Nazirite? The word comes from a verb meaning "to separate or
abstain." Let's learn more about this group of people.

● Numbers 6:2–21 explains in detail the workings of the Nazirite vow.
Copy the following chart into your notebook, and as you read
through this chapter, jot down the requirements for being a Nazirite.
This study will help you understand the backdrop not only of
Samson's life, but also of the lives of Samuel, John the Baptist, and
the Apostle Paul.

The Nazirite Vow	
References	Requirements

6

🖼️ *Living Insights*

Study Two ▬▬▬▬▬▬▬▬▬▬▬▬▬▬▬▬▬▬▬▬▬▬▬▬▬▬▬▬▬▬▬▬

This lesson highlights four principles for us today. If there is a generation that needs to review these principles, it is ours. In your notebook, record your answers to the questions below.

• *Sensuous children can be born of spiritual parents.* Do you agree? Can you think of other biblical examples? How about examples from your acquaintances? What seemed to happen in the lives of these children?

• *A sensuous person focuses on the external rather than on the internal.* Do you fall in love with a body or a person? What's the difference? What part should "good looks" play in developing a relationship?

• *The sensuous life brings one anxiety after another.* Does the media downplay this? Use concrete illustrations. Are you aware of specific anxieties being created by a sensual life? What are they? How can they be dealt with?

• *Sensuality may be dormant, but it is never dead.* Does age have anything to do with sensuous living? If you don't "outgrow" sensual thoughts, how should you deal with them?

Samson: How the
Mighty Are Fallen!

Judges 16:4–31

In Greek mythology Achilles was the son of Peleus, king of the Myrmidons, and Thetis, a sea goddess. Achilles was the greatest, bravest, and most handsome warrior of Agamemnon's army. One of the tales about his childhood relates how Thetis held the young Achilles by the heel and dipped him in the waters of the river Styx. Through the water's mythological power, Achilles became invulnerable—that is, every part except the heel by which he was held. That small portion of his body, untouched by the water, remained vulnerable. From this story we get the term "Achilles' heel," which describes our greatest point of vulnerability. It was at just this point that an arrow struck the near-invincible Achilles and killed him. We all have our "Achilles' heels"—points of extreme vulnerability in our walk with God. For some, it's money; for others, ambition. For Samson, it was sensuality.

I. Samson's Delilah (Judges 16:4–14)

When Samson left the harlot of Gaza (vv. 1–3), he fell into the arms of yet another woman—the infamous Delilah.[1]

> After this it came about that he loved a woman in the valley of Sorek, whose name was Delilah. (v. 4)

The valley of Sorek was the place of the "choice red grape."[2] Certain foods connote to us worlds of description. For example, beans and cornbread suggest *poverty*. Caviar and champagne, on the other hand, suggest *prosperity*. The "choice red grape" connotes *pleasure*. It breathes the enticing bouquet of sensuality. It was in this hedonistic valley that Samson roamed and picked the luscious Delilah from the vine to be his next conquest. The irony, however, was that *he* would end up being conquered—not Delilah.[3] Having a good understanding of Samson's weakness, the Philistines solicited Delilah's help to discover the secret of his strength.

> And the lords of the Philistines came up to her, and said to her, "Entice him, and see where his great strength lies and how we may overpower him that we may bind him to afflict him. Then we will each give you eleven hundred pieces of silver." (v. 5)

---

1. The name Delilah literally means "the weak one" or "the longing one."

2. Alfred Edersheim, *Old Testament Bible History* (Grand Rapids, Mich.: William B. Eerdmans Publishing Co., 1972), vol. 3, p. 174.

3. There is pleasure in sexual sin—at least for a season—but its sweet grapes are quick to ferment and sour. See Proverbs 5:3–5, 6:25–26.

The Hebrew word *entice* means "to find an opening" . . . a point of vulnerability . . . an Achilles' heel. The same word is used earlier when Samson's wife is threatened by the Philistines: *"Entice* your husband, that he may tell us the riddle, lest we burn you and your father's house with fire" (14:15, emphasis added). The word is also used in James 1:14: "But each one is tempted when he is carried away and *enticed* by his own lust" (emphasis added). Here, the Greek word means "luring with bait." It's the picture of a fish that is nestled away, quietly resting underneath a sheltered place. Then a cunning fisherman drops the bait. Whether artificial or real, the bait is designed to appeal to the nature of the fish—to entice. And certain fish are enticed by different baits. For catfish, the fisherman would probably use a treble hook concealed in some form of dough bait or blood bait. For trout, possibly a hand-tied fly or salmon eggs. For Samson, the enticement was the lure of the opposite sex. Like an unsuspecting fish, Samson is drawn out by Delilah, slowly but surely. Naively, the bait is taken, and fatefully, the hook is set. Follow the progression in Proverbs 7:6–23 to see how Samson ended up on Delilah's stringer.

> For at the window of my house
> I looked out through my lattice,
> And I saw among the naive,
> I discerned among the youths,
> A young man lacking sense,
> Passing through the street near her corner;
> And he takes the way to her house,
> In the twilight, in the evening,
> In the middle of the night and in the darkness.
> And behold, a woman comes to meet him,
> Dressed as a harlot and cunning of heart.
> She is boisterous and rebellious;
> Her feet do not remain at home;
> She is now in the streets, now in the squares,
> And lurks by every corner.
> So she seizes him and kisses him,
> And with a brazen face she says to him:
> "I was due to offer peace offerings;
> Today I have paid my vows.
> Therefore I have come out to meet you,
> To seek your presence earnestly, and I have found you.
> I have spread my couch with coverings,
> With colored linens of Egypt.
> I have sprinkled my bed
> With myrrh, aloes and cinnamon.

Come, let us drink our fill of love until morning;
Let us delight ourselves with caresses.
For the man is not at home,
He has gone on a long journey;
He has taken a bag of money with him,
At full moon he will come home."
With her many persuasions she entices him;
With her flattering lips she seduces him.
Suddenly he follows her,
As an ox goes to the slaughter,
Or as one in fetters to the discipline of a fool,
Until an arrow pierces through his liver;
As a bird hastens to the snare,
So he does not know that it will cost him his life.

Blind Spots

It is important to know your strengths. But it is life-or-death *essential* to know your weaknesses. Strengths lead to triumph; weaknesses, to defeat. It was the unprotected heel of Achilles that proved fatal to the mythological hero. And it was Samson's vulnerability to sexual enticement that led to his demise. What is your Achilles' heel? Is it sex . . . greed . . . ambition . . . selfishness . . . drugs . . . alcohol . . . worry . . . anger? Possibly, like Samson, your area of weakness is a blind spot to you. If so, you can bet the aisle seat that the people around you eating popcorn see your weaknesses on a big screen, in 3-D, and in Technicolor. Certainly the Philistines could see Samson's. Why don't you ask a few friends for a candid film review of your life? Remember that "faithful are the wounds of a friend, but deceitful are the kisses of an enemy" (Prov. 27:6). And be thankful that you're surrounded by friends rather than Philistines!

Judges 16:6–14 records Delilah's attempts to unravel the mystery of Samson's strength in order to weaken him for the Philistines. In verses 6, 10, and 13 she questions him, and Samson gives answers that progressively gravitate to the truth: "Bind me with seven fresh cords that have not been dried" (v. 7a); "Bind me tightly with new ropes which have not been used" (v. 11a); "Weave the seven locks of my hair with the web and fasten it" (v. 13a). Frustrated, Delilah poses a final question to Samson, whose answer leads to his demise.

II. Samson's Demise (Judges 16:15–21)

Ironically, the strongest among men is weakened not by soldiers or armies but by one woman. Samson could break the ropes and cords that entwined him but could not extricate himself from the entanglements with Delilah, "the weak one." Samson's cards, which he had held so closely to his chest, are trumped by this persistent woman's final ace: "How can you say 'I love you,' when your heart is not with me?" (v. 15). He folds under pressure in verse 16 and finally reveals his hand in verse 17.

So he told her all that was in his heart and said to her, "A razor has never come on my head, for I have been a Nazirite to God from my mother's womb. If I am shaved, then my strength will leave me and I shall become weak and be like any other man."

Samson's hair was only an outward symbol of his inward commitment to God. Obviously, the latter had eroded to such an extent that the former was no longer sacred to him. In reality, Samson's superhuman strength lay not in his uncut hair but in the mighty presence of God in his life (v. 20). The fall of Samson can be traced to two things: (1) he didn't know his weakness, and (2) he didn't know his strength. Mistakenly, Samson doesn't see God as the real source of his strength. Instead, he sees only himself (see 15:14–17). Consequently, God allows Samson's strength to be taken from him so that in painful circumstances he will learn that without the omnipotent God, he is impotent. As he sleeps, his hair is shaved (v. 19). When he awakes, he is surrounded not by the presence of the Lord but by the revengefully cruel Philistines (v. 20). They seize him, gouge out his eyes, shackle him in bronze chains, and force him to the lowest work a slave in prison could do—grind grain while harnessed to a millstone.

Learning to Lean

In order that we might learn to lean on Him and not on false supports, God removes our crutches—often gently, but sometimes suddenly and without warning. This is exactly what He did with Samson. What about you? Are you trusting in something other than God for your safety, your security, your strength? Possibly you depend more on a portfolio or a financial statement. If so, maybe God will take away that crutch— not so you will fall, but so you will learn, as Samson did, to lean on Him.

The name of the Lord is a strong tower;
The righteous runs into it and is safe.
A rich man's wealth is his strong city,
And like a high wall in his own imagination.
(Prov. 18:10–11)

III. Samson's Death (Judges 16:22–31)

During Samson's dark experience in the dungeon, God's grace began the dim glimmer of a shine. Samson's hair began growing back (v. 22)! As his hair grew, so did his relationship with the Lord. Running his hands through his hair, Samson turned his thoughts and heart back to God. Meanwhile, more than three thousand Philistines had gathered together to offer a great sacrifice to Dagon,[4] their god (vv. 23–24). For entertainment, they summon Samson from prison, amusing themselves with him as he stands between the pillars of the house (vv. 25–27). Standing there, humiliated, he makes a final request of God.

> Then Samson called to the Lord and said, "O Lord God, please remember me and please strengthen me just this time, O God, that I may at once be avenged of the Philistines for my two eyes." And Samson grasped the two middle pillars on which the house rested, and braced himself against them, the one with his right hand and the other with his left. And Samson said, "Let me die with the Philistines!" And he bent with all his might so that the house fell on the lords and all the people who were in it. So the dead whom he killed at his death were more than those whom he killed in his life. (vv. 28–30)

Like Christ, who selflessly died to defeat His enemies of death and the devil, Samson, in an act of self-denial, fulfills his destiny to "begin to deliver Israel from the hands of the Philistines" (13:5b).

A Final Application

With beggar's hands of faith, Samson reaches out to touch the feet of his God: "O Lord God, please remember me. . . ." (16:28). If you're an unbeliever, you can pray with the thief on the cross—"Remember me"—and be assured that you will be with Jesus in paradise (Luke 23:42–43). If you're a believer with a burden, you can pray with the barren Hannah—"Remember me"—and be assured of His compassionate intervention in your circumstances (1 Sam. 1:11–20). If you're a believer who's blown it, you can pray with Samson—"Remember me"—and

---

4. It is debated whether Dagon was a fish-god or a grain-god, but we do know that in Palestine he was the principal deity of the Philistines during the Old Testament period (Judg. 16:23; 1 Sam. 5:2–3, 31:10; 1 Chron. 10:10). Archaeological remains lend support to the accuracy of Judges 16:23–31. Bruce K. Waltke mentions an unearthed Philistine temple at Tel Qasile, "whose artifactual remains, including two pillars separated by a space the length of a very large man's arm span and in front of the altar, comports most favorably with the literary description of [Dagon's] temple at Gaza." *Theological Wordbook of the Old Testament,* ed. R. Laird Harris, Gleason L. Archer, Jr., and Bruce K. Waltke (Chicago, Ill.: Moody Press, 1980), vol. 1, p. 183.

be assured that God's strength can help you overcome your defeated past (Judg. 16:28–30). Maybe somewhere along the line you've forgotten God. The tendency is to think that He, too, has forgotten you. But if the very hairs of your head are numbered, how could He forget *you?* Call to Him, won't you? Whether you're a condemned thief, a burdened Hannah, or a wayward Samson, reach out with hands of faith to touch His feet and heart with the simple prayer—"Remember me."

Living Insights

Study One

Our sinful nature makes resisting the lure of lust a tough job. It's a battle, and that means we need to know our resources, our weapons, and our enemy's strategy. In Proverbs, Solomon passed on a battle plan to his sons. Let's prepare ourselves for battle.

• Copy the chart below into your notebook. Spend some time reading Proverbs 5–7. While you're reading those three chapters, look for four topics: (1) descriptions of the harlot, (2) descriptions of the fool who succumbs to her, (3) descriptions of the wise man who turns away, and (4) practical advice on how to avoid the harlot.

Proverbs 5–7			
The Harlot	The Fool	The Wise Man	Advice

Continued on next page

Living Insights

What a message Samson could have passed on to his children! We can see many of the same thoughts manifested in Solomon's writings to his sons. Let's personalize these concepts in our own lives.

* Write your own version of Proverbs 5–7. You may want to paraphrase certain portions, or you may want to write about *your* feelings as you would convey them to *your* children. Include such matters as admitting and conquering weakness, trifling with sacred things, taking God seriously, and revealing secrets of the heart.

Abigail: A Woman of Wisdom
1 Samuel 25

Hollywood thrives on Cinderella stories with happily-ever-after endings. Deep down inside—regardless of how fairy-taleish they seem—stories like that thrill us because we have this almost genetically coded longing for things to work out happily in the end. A sense of inbred justice causes us to "hiss" Cinderella's cruel and ugly stepsisters and to "hurray" the kind and handsome prince as he sweeps her off her feet. We become wrapped up in the drama because we ourselves are often surrounded by cruel and ugly circumstances. We know how it feels to be on our knees, scrubbing away at heartache until our backs go into spasms and our fingers bleed. Like Cinderella, we long for some charming, princely circumstance to come along and whisk us away from the charwoman's drudgery of life's dirty floors. We are rarely handed Hollywood scripts. First Samuel 25, however, is one such script. The lead actress—Abigail—plays an Academy Award-winning part that is the envy of every woman.

I. The Cast (1 Samuel 25:1–3)

This chapter resembles a three-act play. Following the cast's introductions is the description of the *conflict* on which the plot is centered, escalating action which leads to a *climax,* and a *conclusion* which resolves the conflict. In verses 1–3, the three primary cast members are introduced—David, Nabal, and Abigail.

> Then Samuel died; and all Israel gathered together and mourned for him, and buried him at his house in Ramah. And David arose and went down to the wilderness of Paran. Now there was a man in Maon whose business was in Carmel; and the man was very rich, and he had three thousand sheep and a thousand goats. And it came about while he was shearing his sheep in Carmel (now the man's name was Nabal, and his wife's name was Abigail. And the woman was intelligent and beautiful in appearance, but the man was harsh and evil in his dealings, and he was a Calebite).

The contrast in character between Nabal and Abigail stands out sharply and intensifies the dramatic premise which revolves around the upcoming conflict between David and Nabal.

II. The Conflict (1 Samuel 25:4–13)

David's six hundred men looked after the animals of numerous ranchers in the wilderness of Paran, protecting them from thieves and animals of prey. Payment for the service, like gratuities for waiters, was voluntary. No contracts were written; no words exchanged. But it was understood, like the custom of tipping, that at sheepshearing time a rancher was to pay everyone who had protected his animals (see v. 21). So, David sent ten men to Nabal with a tip tray and these words: "Please give whatever you find at hand to your servants and to your son David" (v. 8). The request was gracious and fair in light of their hospitality and protection (see v. 15). Nabal's miserly, penny-pinching response, however, was far from gracious or fair.

> But Nabal answered David's servants, and said, "Who is David? And who is the son of Jesse? There are many servants today who are each breaking away from his master. Shall I then take my bread and my water and my meat that I have slaughtered for my shearers, and give it to men whose origin I do not know?" (vv. 10–11)

Nabal had sheared many sheep, but David would not be one of them. When David heard from his servants how Nabal tried to fleece them out of their just due, he set out to do a little fleecing of his own—*literally!*

> And David said to his men, "Each of you gird on his sword." So each man girded on his sword. And David also girded on his sword, and about four hundred men went up behind David while two hundred stayed with the baggage. (v. 13)

III. The Climax (1 Samuel 25:14–35)

Meanwhile, back at the ranch, Nabal's wife Abigail was alerted to the situation.

> But one of the young men told Abigail, Nabal's wife, saying, "Behold, David sent messengers from the wilderness to greet our master, and he scorned them. Yet the men were very good to us, and we were not insulted, nor did we miss anything as long as we went about with them, while we were in the fields. They were a wall to us both by night and by day, all the time we were with them tending the sheep. Now therefore, know and consider what you should do, for evil is plotted against our master and against all his household; and he is such a worthless man that no one can speak to him." (vv. 14–17)

Had Abigail reacted like any ordinary woman trapped in an unhappy, mismatched marriage, she might have been tempted to sit back and allow David's vengeance to run its course. After all, Nabal's death would release her from the miserable relationship. But Abigail was no ordinary woman. She steps in, selflessly, to make peace.

> Then Abigail hurried and took two hundred loaves of bread and two jugs of wine and five sheep already prepared and five measures of roasted grain and a hundred clusters of raisins and two hundred cakes of figs, and

16

loaded them on donkeys. And she said to her young men, "Go on before me; behold, I am coming after you." But she did not tell her husband Nabal. And it came about as she was riding on her donkey and coming down by the hidden part of the mountain, that behold, David and his men were coming down toward her; so she met them. (vv. 18–20)

The meeting could have been a fiery clash, but Abigail's humility and honesty doused David's wrath like water on a camp fire.

When Abigail saw David, she hurried and dismounted from her donkey, and fell on her face before David, and bowed herself to the ground. And she fell at his feet and said, "On me alone, my lord, be the blame. And please let your maidservant speak to you, and listen to the words of your maidservant. Please do not let my lord pay attention to this worthless man, Nabal, for as his name is, so is he. Nabal is his name and folly is with him; but I your maidservant did not see the young men of my lord whom you sent. Now therefore, my lord, as the Lord lives, and as your soul lives, since the Lord has restrained you from shedding blood, and from avenging yourself by your own hand, now then let your enemies, and those who seek evil against my lord, be as Nabal. And now let this gift which your maidservant has brought to my lord be given to the young men who accompany my lord. Please forgive the transgression of your maidservant; for the Lord will certainly make for my lord an enduring house, because my lord is fighting the battles of the Lord, and evil shall not be found in you all your days." (vv. 23–28)

In verse 28, Abigail's view of God as the sovereign source of blessing shapes her appeal in verses 29–31 concerning David's reputation, that it might not be marred by this incident. The plea softens David's heart and turns it back to God.

Then David said to Abigail, "Blessed be the Lord God of Israel, who sent you this day to meet me, and blessed be your discernment, and blessed be you, who have kept me this day from bloodshed, and from avenging myself by my own hand. Nevertheless, as the Lord God of Israel lives, who has restrained me from harming you, unless you had come quickly to meet me, surely there would not have been left to Nabal until the morning light as much as one male." So David received from her hand what she had brought him, and he said to her, "Go up to your house in peace. See, I have listened to you and granted your request." (vv. 32–35)

Abigail came to intercede as a peacemaker and left with David's assurance: "Go up to your house in peace" (v. 35a). The blessing bestowed on her by God for being a peacemaker far exceeded her wildest imaginings (Matt. 5:9).

IV. The Conclusion (1 Samuel 25:36–42)

Abigail returns home to find her husband holding a self-indulgent feast where he had become "very drunk" (v. 36). She waits until the next morning to tell him of her encounter with David. Once informed, he is seized with fear and falls into a coma (v. 37). God intervenes ten days later. The Scripture says, "The Lord struck Nabal, and he died" (v. 38). However, the drama doesn't end on a dismal note, but in a fairy-tale fashion.

> When David heard that Nabal was dead, he said, "Blessed be the Lord, who has pleaded the cause of my reproach from the hand of Nabal, and has kept back His servant from evil. The Lord has also returned the evildoing of Nabal on his own head." Then David sent a proposal to Abigail, to take her as his wife.... Then Abigail quickly arose, and rode on a donkey, with her five maidens who attended her; and she followed the messengers of David, and became his wife. (vv. 39–42)

Thus we end our story, as the happy couple rides off into the sunset.

Critic's Choice

As the curtain falls, we feel like giving the drama a standing ovation. Justice is done. Wrong is either righted or forgiven. A bad marriage ends by God's sovereign touch and a new one romantically begins. Cinderella meets her Prince Charming, and we feel assured they will live happily ever after. But what is the critic's review? What can be learned from the drama? I think at least five things.

1. From verse 3: *Differences between husbands and wives do not mean that the marriage cannot continue.* Differences bring not only conflicts but challenges. Sparks may fly on occasion, but as iron sharpens iron, so one person can sharpen another (Prov. 27:17).

2. From verses 17–18: *The wife's primary role is to support her husband.* The woman is to love her man and meet his needs. It is God's responsibility to make him good.

3. From verses 19 and 36: *Silence and timing are two of the most effective ways to handle a strained relationship* (1 Pet. 3:1–2). Abigail's gentle and quiet spirit knew instinctively what to say and when to say it.

---

4. From verse 25: *There is a difference between harsh criticism and honest realism in relating to your mate.* The difference is motive.
5. From verse 39: *God honors the wife who honors her husband* (1 Pet. 3:5–6). In this case, Abigail was relieved of the strain. In some cases, God gives grace to bear the strain.

Living Insights

Study One ▬▬▬▬▬▬▬▬▬▬▬▬▬▬▬▬▬▬▬▬▬▬▬▬▬▬▬▬▬

As we study the life of Abigail, it becomes readily evident that she was a godly woman. She possessed many of the traits that other biblical writers mention when praising qualities of womanhood.

• Copy this chart into your notebook. As you read 1 Samuel 25, write down Abigail's characteristics. Look up other passages (Gen. 2, Eph. 5, 1 Pet. 3) and note which of her traits are actually stated as principles in complementary Scripture.

References	Abigail's Traits	References	Godly Women's Traits

Living Insights

Study Two ▬▬▬▬▬▬▬▬▬▬▬▬▬▬▬▬▬▬▬▬▬▬▬▬▬▬▬▬▬

In Abigail we see a rare blend of feminine ingenuity and wifely support of her husband. What a winning combination! If you're a wife, where do you rate in these categories? If you're a husband, how's your attitude when it comes to your relationship with your wife? Do you fit in a "Nabal" category?

Continued on next page

19

- Take this little quiz. Check (√) the appropriate box.
  1. Differences between husbands and wives do not mean the marriage cannot continue.
     - ☐ Disagree
     - ☐ Not Sure
     - ☐ Agree but Doesn't Apply
     - ☐ Agree and Applies
  2. The wife's primary role is to support her husband.
     - ☐ Disagree
     - ☐ Not Sure
     - ☐ Agree but Doesn't Apply
     - ☐ Agree and Applies
  3. Silence and timing are two of the most effective ways to handle a strained relationship.
     - ☐ Disagree
     - ☐ Not Sure
     - ☐ Agree but Doesn't Apply
     - ☐ Agree and Applies
  4. There is a difference between harsh criticism and honest realism in relating to your mate.
     - ☐ Disagree
     - ☐ Not Sure
     - ☐ Agree but Doesn't Apply
     - ☐ Agree and Applies
  5. God honors the wife who honors her husband.
     - ☐ Disagree
     - ☐ Not Sure
     - ☐ Agree but Doesn't Apply
     - ☐ Agree and Applies
- Now sit down with your mate—or if unmarried, with a close friend—and discuss the "why" behind your answers.

Absalom: The Rebel Prince Charming

2 Samuel 13–18

From "Dallas" to "Dynasty," nighttime soap operas are seething cauldrons of power, greed, lust, adultery, intrigue, and treachery. Nothing is sacred; no one is safe. Everything and everyone is up for grabs. It's survival of the fittest, on both a personal and a corporate level. It's a dog-eat-dog world, and the puppies don't make it. In these jungles of tangled family relationships, brother is pitted against brother, wife against husband, father against son. Such is the stuff that television melodrama is made of. But scripts like these are not the inventions of imaginative writers fertile with fantasy; they originate in real life, with real people. One such family feud is found in 2 Samuel, where a son's imprisoned bitterness toward his father breaks its fetters, allowing rebellion and revenge to run loose, unrestrained. And since this was the king's son, not only was the king endangered but also the kingdom itself. This royal family lived in a fishbowl, and their drama became nightly viewing for the entire nation. Sex, murder, cover-ups, ambitions, political intrigue, power struggles—they had enough plots, subplots, and counterplots to fill seasons of programming on every major network. Were it a television drama, the family's story might be titled simply "Israel" or "Kingdom," for the story is centered on David, the greatest king in Israel's history. Of course, the advertising hype boasts a cast of thousands, but for this episode, the main stars—listed in alphabetical order—are Absalom and David.

I. Absalom's Home (2 Samuel 3:2–5, 5:13–16)

David's immediate family tree, from which sprouted the rotten fruit of Absalom, resembles an overgrown peach orchard: seven wives in Hebron and an unnumbered amount of wives and concubines in Jerusalem. With his wives alone, David fathered twenty sons and one daughter.[1] With boughs weighed down so heavily, it is no wonder that some of the offspring would fall from the tree to rot underneath its very branches. Such was the case with Absalom. But the finger of blame cannot be pointed solely at the young rebel. Because of his father's polygamy, Absalom grew up in a fragmented home. Also, Absalom saw within his home some incomprehensible inconsistencies in David's life. However, the passing of years covers a multitude of sins for history's heroes. Now we look upon David with awe and admiration. The headlines we remember are: "Shepherd Boy Slays Giant" ... "War Hero Becomes King" ... "David: A Man after God's Own Heart." On every street corner, newsboys called out

---

1. See 2 Samuel 3:2–5, 13–14, 5:14–16; 1 Chronicles 3:5–9; 2 Chronicles 11:18.

"Read all about it!" and boasted their king's exploits. However, at home, Absalom got the inside scoop on his father's life. In his formative years, Absalom was part of a fragmented family fraught with rivalry and rife with court gossip. Old enough to understand, Absalom witnessed his father's involvement with Bathsheba and the ensuing cover-up that makes Watergate look like a child's game of hide-and-seek.[2]

A Child's Eyes

In Arthur Miller's *Death of a Salesman,* the traveling salesman Willy Loman is idolized by his teenage son, Biff. Although Willy was on the road a lot, Biff held him in the highest esteem. Everything the boy did in life was to please his father, whether it was playing football or applying to college. But one day Biff stumbled upon his father having an affair with another woman—and all that changed. For the first time he saw the man behind the mask. Biff was crushed . . . devastated. From that time on, Biff's relationship with his father changed drastically. Hurt grew roots of bitterness deep within his heart and choked the relationship with his father. The sudden unveiling of hypocrisy before a child's eyes produces such results. It did with Biff. It did with Absalom. May I get painfully personal with you for a moment? What story is your family reading about your life? Are they buying the journalistic hype at the newsstand, or are they doing some investigative reporting of their own behind the scenes? What, then, are they uncovering—honesty or hypocrisy? You can expend a lot of energy—as David and Willy Loman did—in covering up, or you can channel that energy into living your life in such a way that a cover-up isn't necessary. Remember, your life—front page, sports page, comics—is being read by impressionable eyes. Eyes that don't easily forgive *or* forget.

II. Absalom's Bitterness (2 Samuel 13:1–14:24)

Professionally, David was enmeshed in the affairs of state and diplomacy. Domestically, with all his wives, concubines, and children, what time he had at home was spread far too thin to be effective. It is no surprise that in jumping from chapter 3 to chapter 13—a leap of twenty years—no mention is made of Absalom. He's simply overlooked by the biblical writer, which undoubtedly was what

---

2. Read the inside news of David's clandestine sexual charades, the murderous cover-up, and the public scandal in 2 Samuel 11–12.

happened in his relationship with David. He was simply *overlooked* by a father who was either too busy or too tired for too long.

Little Things, Overlooked

It is easy to overlook little things, especially when it comes to your children. Too tired to play ball when you get home from work, you overlook the fact that your child has waited all day—which for a child seems an eternity—for you to come home. Too busy with work taken home from the office or with domestic chores, you overlook reading the bedtime story or tucking the children into bed. Too enmeshed in the newspaper or your favorite TV program, you overlook the fact that your child is struggling with a confusing homework assignment and could really use your help. Little things, overlooked. In his *Poor Richard's Almanac,* Benjamin Franklin shows the importance of little things and how disastrous it can be when they are overlooked.

> For want of a nail the shoe was lost; for want of a shoe the horse was lost; and for want of a horse the rider was lost; being overtaken and slain by the enemy, all for want of care about a horseshoe nail.[3]

A. Amnon's violation of Tamar (13:1–22). An incident that further deepened Absalom's bitterness toward his father is described in chapter 13. David's oldest son, Amnon, had fallen in love with his half sister, Tamar, who was Absalom's sister. Through subterfuge Amnon was able to get the girl alone and raped her (vv. 1–14). After his sexual appetite was sated, Amnon's feelings toward the girl changed. We read that "the hatred with which he hated her was greater than the love with which he had loved her" (v. 15). Tamar fled, hurt and humiliated, to stay with Absalom (v. 20). King David heard of Amnon's crime and became "very angry" (v. 21), but there is no record of any reprimand.[4] It was an unpleasant incident and David wanted it kept out of the papers, so he swept the dirt under the family rug. Undoubtedly, this failure to act further fueled the fires of Absalom's burning hatred toward his dad.

B. Absalom's revenge against Amnon (13:23–39, 14:1–23). After two years of his revenge simmering on the back burner,

---

3. Benjamin Franklin in *Five Thousand Quotations for All Occasions,* ed. Lewis C. Henry (Garden City, N.Y.: Doubleday and Co., 1945), p. 28.

4. The Mosaic Law clearly states that such an offense is an abomination and that the offender should be disciplined by being cut off from the nation (Lev. 18).

bsalom inflames a plot to murder Amnon. With David's approval, Absalom arranges for Amnon to take the grand tour of his sheepshearing enterprise in Baal-hazor. However, under this facade of friendliness, Absalom brews a covert plot that he delegates to his servants: "See now, when Amnon's heart is merry with wine, and when I say to you, 'Strike Amnon,' then put him to death. Do not fear; have not I myself commanded you? Be courageous and be valiant" (v. 28). With the plot unfolding like the structured scenes of a Hollywood murder mystery, Amnon is killed, and Absalom flees for three years to hide with his grandfather, Talmai, king of Geshur. Eventually, Absalom is recalled to Jerusalem, resettled but not reconciled to his father (14:1–23).

III. Absalom's Popularity (2 Samuel 14:25–26)

Verses 25–26 give us a glimpse of Absalom's physical appearance and popularity.

> Now in all Israel was no one as handsome as Absalom, so highly praised; from the sole of his foot to the crown of his head there was no defect in him. And when he cut the hair of his head (and it was at the end of every year that he cut it, for it was heavy on him so he cut it), he weighed the hair of his head at 200 shekels by the king's weight.

IV. Absalom's Conspiracy (2 Samuel 14:28–17:29)

The motive and method of Absalom's conspiracy against David bubbled to the surface during the two years he resided, estranged from his father, in Jerusalem.

A. Absalom's motive (vv. 28–33). For two years, Absalom has been allowed to live in Jerusalem but not allowed to see his father (vv. 21–24). In a play-me-or-trade-me gesture, Absalom forces Joab, one of David's men, to negotiate a meeting with him and his father: " 'Now therefore, let me see the king's face; and if there is iniquity in me, let him put me to death' " (v. 32b). A meeting is arranged. Absalom prostrates himself before the king, and the king kisses him. The scene has all the external staging of a reconciliation, but something is missing. Both men seem to be playing out contrived roles—acting out parts—rather than reacting with genuine emotion. Undoubtedly, Absalom no longer looks to David as a father with whom to be reconciled, but a foe to be reckoned with.

B. Absalom's method (15:1–16:23). With his personal charm (14:25) and political charisma (15:1–5), "Absalom stole away the hearts of the men of Israel" (v. 6). Cunningly, he uses his influence to construct his own cabinet with men who had defected from David's circle of leadership (v. 12). The ground swell conspiracy rippled through the palace right under David's nose. Suddenly caught in the vortex of a *coup d'état,* David and his servants flee the palace (vv. 13–14). As a personal affront to his father, Absalom went in to the royal harem, which David had left behind, and had sex with them on the same porch where David had had relations with Bathsheba (16:20–23).

V. Absalom's Death (2 Samuel 18:1–33)

As David organized an army to recapture Jerusalem, he ordered his men to deal gently with Absalom. Meanwhile, Absalom, riding under an overgrown oak tree, got his long hair entangled in its branches and was left hanging helplessly in midair. Finding Absalom in the tree, Joab drove three spears into his heart. In spite of the fact that this proverbial burr in David's saddle had been removed, wounds of regret remained, goading his conscience. Hearing the news of Absalom's death, David responds with the greatest remorse.

> And the king was deeply moved and went up to the chamber over the gate and wept. And thus he said as he walked, "O my son Absalom, my son, my son Absalom! Would I had died instead of you, O Absalom, my son, my son!" (18:33)

VI. Some Concluding Applications

The story of Absalom's relationship with his father is a tragic one, but we can learn some valuable lessons through their painful mistakes.

A. An unhappy home breeds unbalanced children. It does bear true that we reap what we sow—even what we don't sow. Where wheat isn't planted, tares of indulgence grow in its place, making for a backbreaking harvest. Are you cultivating a happy home, or are you too tired or too busy to sow the right kind of seed (see Prov. 24:30–34)? Remember, if you sow nothing, you can expect to reap only weeds.

B. An undisciplined family breeds insecurity and resentment. We have no record of David ever disciplining his children for their many wrongs. Children need boundaries enforced to give them a sense of security. They need a degree of freedom, but only within the secure grounds provided by well-constructed fences. When children cut holes in the fences you have erected, and you fail to hold them accountable by bringing them back and mending the fences, they question your love for them (Prov. 13:24). Eventually, this leads to resentment, and ultimately, to rebellion.

C. An unreconciled relationship breeds sores that never heal. Even the death of the resented person can't stanch the flow of ill feelings. Unreconciled hurt has a way of reaching out from the grave and wagging its bony finger at the one still living.

25

Forgiveness is the only way to restore estranged relationships—
not geographical separation or even death. Paul's advice here
is timely.

> Let all bitterness and wrath and anger and clamor
> and slander be put away from you, along with all
> malice. And be kind to one another, tender-hearted,
> forgiving each other, just as God in Christ also has
> forgiven you. (Eph. 4:31–32)

Living Insights

Study One

The old saying goes, Like father, like son. Does Absalom remind you
of his dad? Let's walk through some territory in 2 Samuel with the
express purpose of comparing and contrasting.

- Copy the chart below into your notebook. As you read 2 Samuel 3
  and 13–18, jot down characteristics of these men. In each instance,
  ask yourself, Is this trait seen in both men? Or is it a contrast? Check
  (√) the appropriate column.

David				Absalom			
Verses	Characteristics	Compare (√)	Contrast (√)	Verses	Characteristics	Compare (√)	Contrast (√)

Living Insights

Study Two

Some very timely and practical lessons emerge from this study of family
relationships. Let's spend time on each one. You may want to do this together as a family, in a study group, or alone. We're personalizing here . . .
jumping right out of the study guide into *your* life.

- *An unhappy home breeds unbalanced children.* Do you agree? Can you think of illustrations you've observed? Share them. What are some definite ways you can contribute to making your home happy? Name a few.
- *An undisciplined family breeds insecurity and resentment.* What priority do luxury and leisure have in your home? How is discipline handled in your home? If you had to pinpoint a weak area in your discipline, what would it be? During this next week, how can you work on your weakness?
- *An unreconciled relationship breeds sores that never heal.* How would you rate your family relationships? Have they been suffering due to "busyness"? List three ways you can resolve this problem right away. Close by asking God for strength to follow through on your plans.

Rehoboam: The Reckless Phony
1 Kings 11–14

With a dazzling array of movie stars, expensive sets, and special effects, the movie industry makes its living by manufacturing illusions—making something phony look real. The words *lights . . . camera . . . action* introduce us to an artificial world constructed from scripts, actors, rehearsals, veneered sets, and special lighting. It's all contrived to create a sense of reality. But true reality does not end up on the reels of 35-mm film to be shown in the theater. True reality takes place off camera, behind the scenes. For example, the 1939 classic film *The Wizard of Oz* created a host of illusions that simulated reality: the tornado that threatened Dorothy's farm . . . the uprooting of the farmhouse into the vortex of the tornado . . . the Wicked Witch's army of winged monkeys flying through the air. From our point of view these all seem real, but from the other side of the camera we get a picture of the behind-the-scenes reality. The tornado was created by attaching a huge muslin sock to a movable steel structure at the top, and at the bottom to a small car that would zigzag back and forth to pull the tip of the huge sock through a slot in the stage floor. To heighten the illusion, fuller's earth and compressed air were fed into the sock from the bottom with air hoses. The porous muslin let enough of the fuller's earth through to create a cloud of dust that disguised the sock. The model of the farmhouse used in the tornado sequence was just three feet tall. First, the house was photographed falling on a floor painted to look like the sky. Then, to create the illusion that the tornado was picking up the house, the film was run backward. And the threatening army of monkeys? Most were an intimidating six inches high, cast in rubber, and hung by piano wire one-thousandth of an inch thick. There were only about a dozen real people dressed in monkey costumes, suspended on somewhat thicker wire. Underneath their monkey suits were small battery-driven electric motors adapted from windshield wiper motors that made the wings go up and down.[1] Sitting in a darkened theater and seeing the moviemaker's finished product, it's difficult to spot the socks and piano wires of special effects. However, when we go behind the scenes—off camera—it's easy to spot what's phony and what's real. In this study, we're going to take a Universal Studios Tour on the back lots of a man named Rehoboam, to see what's for real and what's phony about his life.

I. The Roots of Rehoboam's Phoniness (1 Kings 11)

You don't have to trace Rehoboam's genealogical roots very far to find the source of his on-camera, off-camera, duplicitous life. Rehoboam's father was Solomon, and his mother was Naamah, a

---

1. Taken from *The Making of the Wizard of Oz,* by Aljean Harmetz (New York, N.Y.: Alfred A. Knopf, 1981).

distinguished Ammonite woman.[2] Undoubtedly, Rehoboam had read his father's Song of Songs, which extolled the sanctity and beauty of the marriage relationship. However, Solomon's seven hundred wives and three hundred concubines surely revealed a discrepancy between what he published and what went on in his private life (v. 3). In order to make his royal marriages effective, Solomon thought it necessary to build temples for the more important wives living with him in Jerusalem (vv. 5–8). International marriages commonly required the recognition of foreign deities, and Solomon's were no exception. As a result, these wives "turned his heart away after other gods" (v. 4). Again, Rehoboam saw in his father a dual standard: confessing one God, yet tolerating the influential presence of many foreign gods. Finally, raised on his father's Proverbs, which stressed wisdom and self-discipline, Rehoboam saw Solomon living out the experiences of a self-indulgent fool as recorded, autobiographically, in Ecclesiastes. When Solomon died, Rehoboam succeeded him at the age of forty-one (v. 43). His first decision as head of state revealed his two-sided character.

II. The Examples of Rehoboam's Phoniness

Four incidents in Rehoboam's reign serve to strip the veneer of righteousness that overlaid his life and reveal the cheap, splintered plywood of wickedness. For forty-one years Rehoboam had lived in his father's shadow, where he learned to play a rehearsed role for the public eye, all the while nurturing—behind the scenes, away from the camera—a life of self-indulgence and expediency.

A. The incident regarding taxation (12:1–20). Upon Rehoboam's taking the throne, the people come to him with a request.

> "Your father made our yoke hard; therefore lighten the
> hard service of your father and his heavy yoke which
> he put on us, and we will serve you." (v. 4)

Rehoboam sent them away for three days in order to take the matter under advisement.

> And King Rehoboam consulted with the elders who
> had served his father Solomon while he was still
> alive, saying, "How do you counsel me to answer this
> people?" Then they spoke to him, saying, "If you will be

---

2. The Ammonites were descendants of Lot's youngest daughter. She lived in Sodom, where all the sensual cults of illicit sex, along with the pagan gods Molech and Milcom, had their roots. Worship of these deities involved sacrificing children in a furnace of fire. "Excavations in Palestine have uncovered piles of ashes and remains of infant skeletons in cemeteries around heathen altars, pointing to the widespread practice of this cruel abomination." Merrill F. Unger, *Archaeology and the Old Testament* (Grand Rapids, Mich.: Zondervan Publishing House, 1970), p. 279.

> a servant to this people today, will serve them, grant
> them their petition, and speak good words to them,
> then they will be your servants forever." (vv. 6–7)

Although Rehoboam went through the motions of seeking counsel from his father's veteran advisers, he rejected their advice
and turned to his peers.

> So he said to them, "What counsel do you give that
> we may answer this people who have spoken to me,
> saying, 'Lighten the yoke which your father put on
> us'?" And the young men who grew up with him
> spoke to him, saying, "Thus you shall say to this
> people who spoke to you, saying, 'Your father made
> our yoke heavy, now you make it lighter for us!' But
> you shall speak to them, 'My little finger is thicker
> than my father's loins! Whereas my father loaded you
> with a heavy yoke, I will add to your yoke; my father
> disciplined you with whips, but I will discipline you
> with scorpions.[3] " (vv. 9–11)

Verse 15 states that "the king did not listen to the people." Deep
down inside, Rehoboam had no intention of giving ear to the
needs of the people. As a result, civil war ensued (vv. 16–24).
The ten tribes of the north revolted and established a separate
nation under the name Israel, making Jeroboam their leader.
Rehoboam was left with only two tribes, Judah and Benjamin,
forming the nation of Judah.

B. The incident regarding civil war (2 Chron. 11). Through
a man named Shemaiah, God told Rehoboam not to fight against
his relatives in the northern kingdom.

> " 'Thus says the Lord, "You shall not go up or fight
> against your relatives; return every man to his house,
> for this thing is from Me." ' " So they listened to the
> words of the Lord and returned from going against
> Jeroboam. (v. 4)

On camera, Rehoboam appears obedient. But off camera, he
actually beefs up his country's defenses for war.

> Rehoboam lived in Jerusalem and built cities for
> defense in Judah. Thus he built Bethlehem, Etam,
> Tekoa, Beth-zur, Soco, Adullam, Gath, Mareshah,
> Ziph, Adoraim, Lachish, Azekah, Zorah, Aijalon, and
> Hebron, which are fortified cities in Judah and in
> Benjamin. He also strengthened the fortresses and

---

3. The scorpion referred to here was a lash that had a single handle but nine to twelve leather
straps embedded with pieces of bone or metal. The whip was only a wooden handle with a
single leather strap.

put officers in them and stores of food, oil and wine.
And he put shields and spears in every city and
strengthened them greatly. So he held Judah and
Benjamin. (vv. 5–12)

Hardly the picture of someone relaxing and trusting God. Behind
the scenes, he was aggressively building his national defense
system: fortifying key cities, strengthening fortresses with officers and supplies, and building an arsenal of weapons.

C. **The incident regarding the capital city** (1 Kings 14:21–24).
On the surface, Jerusalem looked as if it were the city of the
Lord. In reality, it had become the city of Naamah, Rehoboam's
Ammonite mother.

Now Rehoboam the son of Solomon reigned in Judah.
Rehoboam was forty-one years old when he became
king, and he reigned seventeen years in Jerusalem,
the city which the Lord had chosen from all the tribes
of Israel to put His name there. And his mother's
name was Naamah the Ammonitess. And Judah did
evil in the sight of the Lord, and they provoked Him
to jealousy more than all that their fathers had done,
with the sins which they committed. For they also
built for themselves high places and sacred pillars
and Asherim on every high hill and beneath every
luxuriant tree. And there were also male cult prosti-
tutes in the land. They did according to all the abomi-
nations of the nations which the Lord dispossessed
before the sons of Israel. (vv. 21–24)

When Solomon brought his pagan wives into the city, he erected
altars and effigies to their gods. Apparently, Naamah's influence
exceeded that of his other wives. The sensuality and human
sacrifice that accompanied her form of worship brought abomi-
nable conditions to Jerusalem. On the surface, Jerusalem bore
the Lord's name. It was His city. However, the city, like Rehoboam, was really a whitewashed tomb, full of death and decay.

D. **The incident regarding Solomon's shields** (2 Chron.
12:1–12). Because of Rehoboam's unfaithfulness to Him, God led
the king of Egypt, Shishak, against Jerusalem. This resulted in
the pillage of both the Lord's house and the king's palace. Following the plunder, Rehoboam's character again shows through
his shallow facade.

So Shishak king of Egypt came up against Jerusalem,
and took the treasures of the house of the Lord and
the treasures of the king's palace. He took everything;
he even took the golden shields which Solomon had

made. Then King Rehoboam made shields of bronze in their place, and committed them to the care of the commanders of the guard who guarded the door of the king's house. And it happened as often as the king entered the house of the Lord, the guards came and carried them and then brought them back into the guards' room. (vv. 9–11)

First Kings 10 catalogs the vast array of opulent wealth that Solomon had in his palace. Regarding the shields, he had made "200 large shields of beaten gold, using 600 shekels of gold on each large shield. And he made 300 shields of beaten gold, using three minas of gold on each shield" (vv. 16–17a). In hopes that the public wouldn't discover the theft, Rehoboam cleverly arranged for shields made out of bronze to replace the gold ones. He worked surreptitiously behind the scenes to cover up the loss, and through his special effects department, managed to make the phony bronze substitutes seem like the real thing. To strengthen the illusion, he kept the shields from close public view. Another example of his hypocrisy and phoniness.

E. A brief summary. In conclusion, we see four areas of hypocrisy in Rehoboam's life. He said he sought counsel, but he never really listened to the people. He said he would not fight, but behind the scenes he was fortifying his cities for battle. He lived in a city that was to have the name of the Lord, but it actually had the name of his mother Naamah, a worshiper of pagan gods. Finally, he sought to cover up the loss of the stolen gold shields by replacing them with stand-ins made of bronze. In these four scenes we see Rehoboam as a consummate actor skilled at performances aimed to please the public eye.

Personal Application

The word *hypocrite* comes from the Greek word *hupokritēs,* which is an old word for "actor" that described a character on the ancient Greek stage who wore a mask as he recited his lines. It's easy to live a theatrical, on-camera existence, like Rehoboam, aimed at pleasing the public, while our off-camera, behind-the-scenes life is full of self-indulgence and deception. But though we may fool the audience, we will never fool the Lord. He will always be the Critic who sees behind our masks and into our hearts.

> "Woe to you, scribes and Pharisees, hypocrites! For you are like whitewashed tombs which on the outside appear beautiful, but inside they are full of dead men's bones and all uncleanness.

Even so you too outwardly appear righteous to men, but inwardly you are full of hypocrisy and lawlessness." (Matt. 23:27–28)

If you're living an on-stage, off-stage double life, remember that in the balcony sits a Critic whose Word cuts through the fluff of your pretended role and pierces "as far as the division of soul and spirit, of both joints and marrow, and [is] able to judge the thoughts and intentions of the heart. And there is no creature hidden from His sight, but all things are open and laid bare to [His] eyes" (Heb. 4:12–13).

Living Insights

Study One

Rehoboam had the outward appearance of having it all together. But a closer look reveals that inside it was all falling apart. Let's take a closer look at this man's life.

- Take some time to read 1 Kings 11–14. Get a perspective on Rehoboam's life and reign, and try to put his life into a detailed outline. Follow it through to his death in 14:31. After you've completed the outline, put a check (√) by everything in the outline that was fake, phony—surface stuff. Does anything you've found hit home in your life? Talk with God about this study.

Living Insights

Study Two

It's one thing to *read* about a phony. It's quite another thing to *be* one. Have you given it much thought recently? Let's do that.

- Who are you? Do you have a public life and a private life? How different are they? Make a copy of the chart below and fill it in. What can you learn about yourself? Circle a specific area you can work on this week. Complete this chart slowly and thoughtfully.

Your Name	
What Others See	What God Sees

33

Naaman and Gehazi: Characters in Contrast

2 Kings 5

Poetic justice is a literary term first introduced in England by Thomas Rymer in 1678. It denotes that the characters in a drama essentially reap the harvest of what they sow—for the virtuous, reward; for the wicked, punishment. It can be easily seen in Nahum Tate's 1681 revision of Shakespeare's most pessimistic work, *King Lear.* In his revision, Tate deletes the character of the Fool and adds a happy ending. The villains die and the heroes live. Lear is restored to his throne, and Cordelia weds Edgar. In 2 Kings 5, a similar type of drama is enacted that forever changes the courses of two men's lives. The men: Naaman and Gehazi. The first was a leper; the second, a servant of God's prophet Elisha. In an example of poetic justice, a surprising change takes place in the lives of both men. The leper becomes a servant of God; the servant, in turn, becomes a leper. As the curtain rises on this drama, we'll be able to see Naaman and Gehazi with front-row clarity. And all the character lines etching their faces will be revealed as the footlights of God's Word wash over them. We'll see that both faces are lined and shadowed with unbelief, which in Naaman manifests itself as pride and in Gehazi as greed.

I. Naaman (2 Kings 5:1–14)

A. Descriptions of Naaman (v. 1). In the opening credits, Naaman is described in glowing terms.

> Now Naaman, captain of the army of the king of Aram,
> was a great man with his master, and highly respected,
> because by him the Lord had given victory to Aram.
> The man was also a valiant warrior, but he was a leper.[1]

Naaman was a high-ranking officer in the Syrian army. His war record was impressive: instrumental in bringing peace in the land. His personal references were impeccable: "a great man with his master, and highly respected." And, not only was he a great military leader, he was also a "valiant warrior" himself—something like a highly respected player-coach. However, one physical flaw dogged Naaman's every footstep: *he was a leper.*

---

1. Leprosy is "a slowly progressing and intractable disease characterized by subcutaneous nodules . . . , scabs or cuticular crusts . . . and white shining spots appearing to be deeper than the skin. . . . The disease is a zymotic affection produced by a microbe discovered by Hansen in 1871. It is contagious, although not very readily communicated by casual contact. . . . [In] those forms in which nodular growths are the most prominent features . . . the limbs often drop off." *The International Standard Bible Encyclopaedia,* gen. ed. James Orr (Grand Rapids, Mich.: William B. Eerdmans Publishing Co., 1976), vol. 3, p. 1867.

Leprosy in biblical times was a dreaded skin disease. Those who had it, at least in Israel, were outcasts of society. They were often banished to live in colonies, ostracized by the community (Lev. 13, especially vv. 45–46). Although Syrian social regulations were not as stringent as Israel's, the diseased skin of a leper was a stigma that shadowed the person all through life. It was a disease that could be pronounced cleansed by the priest but could not be cured (Lev. 14).

B. **Events leading to Naaman's cure** (vv. 2–14). Even before Naaman's conversion, God was at work coupling together a chain of events that would lead to the cure of his leprosy, "because by him the Lord had given victory" (v. 1). Coming to verse 2, we see a small but indispensable link in that chain.

> Now the Arameans had gone out in bands, and had taken captive a little girl from the land of Israel; and she waited on Naaman's wife. And she said to her mistress, "I wish that my master were with the prophet who is in Samaria! Then he would cure him of his leprosy." (vv. 2–3)

A "little girl," yet mightily used by God to set Naaman on a life-changing course to leprosy's cure. The next link in God's chain of events is a bigger one—Naaman's master, the king of Aram.

> And Naaman went in and told his master, saying, "Thus and thus spoke the girl who is from the land of Israel." Then the king of Aram said, "Go now, and I will send a letter to the king of Israel." And he departed and took with him ten talents of silver and six thousand shekels of gold and ten changes of clothes. (vv. 4–5)

Notice Naaman's thinking as an unbeliever. The first thing that comes to his mind is, "I'll give money. I'll buy my cure." So, with Gucci bags full of gold, garment bags stuffed with a valuable collection of designer clothes, and a letter of entrée, he sets off with the wind of optimism in his sails.

> And he brought the letter to the king of Israel, saying, "And now as this letter comes to you, behold, I have sent Naaman my servant to you, that you may cure him of his leprosy." And it came about when the king of Israel read the letter, that he tore his clothes and said, "Am I God, to kill and to make alive, that this man is sending word to me to cure a man of his leprosy? But consider now, and see how he is seeking a quarrel against me." (vv. 6–7)

The request literally tears the king of Israel to pieces with its superhuman demands. He replies, exasperated: "Am I God?..." Upon reflection, the king imagines that the request might be some ploy to create an incident between the two kingdoms. Fortunately for the king, the matter reaches Elisha's ears and is immediately delegated to him.

> And it happened when Elisha the man of God heard
> that the king of Israel had torn his clothes, that he
> sent word to the king, saying, "Why have you torn
> your clothes? Now let him come to me, and he shall
> know that there is a prophet in Israel." (v. 8)

Naaman wastes no time beating a direct path to the prophet's door.

> So Naaman came with his horses and his chariots,
> and stood at the doorway of the house of Elisha. And
> Elisha sent a messenger to him, saying, "Go and wash
> in the Jordan seven times, and your flesh shall be
> restored to you and you shall be clean."[2] (vv. 9–10)

Once the entourage reaches Elisha's house, Naaman is greeted in a manner that seems to him totally inhospitable and humiliating. First, he is not invited in but is left to stand in Elisha's doorway. Second, Elisha doesn't come to greet him but only sends his messenger. Third, the prescription the messenger brings hardly fits the bill of what Naaman had expected from so great a prophet as Elisha. For a man who had been accustomed to buying everything he wanted, the prescription was a hard pill to swallow. Try to envision the emotional backdrop. Here is a man more used to giving orders than taking them, more used to paying his own way than receiving gifts. Here is a man who had traveled a long way and had just come from an emotionally wrenching reception with Israel's king. He had just ridden nonstop to the probably remote, out-of-the-way home of some foreign religious fanatic. But to his chagrin, he is greeted with humiliation instead of hospitality. Standing at the doorway with his entourage looking on, he reads this little crumpled-up note given him by Elisha's servant. And, if it wasn't bad enough for a Syrian to come to a Jew's land, he was expected to do some silly ritual dip in the muddy Jordan river. Understanding the background and Naaman's pride, his reply is predictable.

> But Naaman was furious and went away and said,
> "Behold, I thought, 'He will surely come out to me,

---

2. Elisha's prescription is reminiscent of Leviticus 14:1–8, yet without all the trappings of ceremonial detail.

and stand and call on the name of the Lord his God, and wave his hand over the place, and cure the leper.' Are not Abanah and Pharpar, the rivers of Damascus, better than all the waters of Israel? Could I not wash in them and be clean?" So he turned and went away in a rage. (vv. 11–12)

Then, just as Naaman threatened to break the chain, another minor link holds the events leading to his cure in place.

Then his servants came near and spoke to him and said, "My father, had the prophet told you to do some great thing, would you not have done it? How much more then, when he says to you, 'Wash, and be clean'?" (v. 13)

In spite of his rage, Naaman realizes that the servant's reasoning is right and reacts more rationally.

So he went down and dipped himself seven times in the Jordan, according to the word of the man of God; and his flesh was restored like the flesh of a little child, and he was clean. (v. 14)

An Observation about Naaman

In Naaman's defense, we can't overlook the fact that he listened to the advice of those under him—the little servant girl (vv. 2–3), Elisha's servant (v. 10), his own servants (v. 13). God sometimes works in strange ways to bring about His will. He speaks through His Word (Heb. 4:12), but He also speaks through the whirlwind (Job 38:1). He speaks through the prophets (Heb. 1:1), but He also speaks through Balaam's donkey (Num. 22:28). It appears, then, that the only way to hear all that God has to say to us is to develop a listening ear and a learning heart. Proverbs instructs us that "in abundance of counselors there is victory" (11:14b). Like some of the Old Testament prophets, those counselors can occasionally come in strange garb— a sunset . . . a psalm . . . a sparrow . . . even a servant. How are your ears? Have you been in for a hearing test lately— or should I say a *listening* test? Try listening to and learning from a little child—as Naaman did. If you can pass that first test, God is beginning to train your ears to hear His footsteps, soft but certain amid the traffic of everyday life.

II. Gehazi (2 Kings 5:15–27)

Verses 15–19 form a literary bridge by which Naaman and Gehazi are brought together. Elated with his cleansing, Naaman rushes to thank Elisha and makes a genuine profession of faith: "Behold now, I know that there is no God in all the earth, but in Israel" (v. 15). Then, he not only urges Elisha to accept a present of gratitude but upon Elisha's refusal, he urges him again. Meanwhile, standing in the shadows, Elisha's servant Gehazi overhears this volley of offers and refusals. You can almost hear the dollar signs ringing in his head as he tabulates the profit.

> But Gehazi, the servant of Elisha the man of God, thought,
> "Behold, my master has spared this Naaman the Aramean,
> by not receiving from his hands what he brought. As the
> Lord lives, I will run after him and take something from
> him." (v. 20)

Seizing an opportunity for financial gain, Gehazi slips out the back to catch up to Naaman.

> So Gehazi pursued Naaman. When Naaman saw one run-
> ning after him, he came down from the chariot to meet
> him and said, "Is all well?" (v. 21)

It is at this point that Gehazi's imagination sprouts full blooms of colorful lies.

> And he said, "All is well. My master has sent me, saying,
> 'Behold, just now two young men of the sons of the proph-
> ets have come to me from the hill country of Ephraim.
> Please give them a talent of silver and two changes of
> clothes.'" And Naaman said, "Be pleased to take two tal-
> ents." And he urged him, and bound two talents of silver
> in two bags with two changes of clothes, and gave them
> to two of his servants; and they carried them before him.
> (vv. 22–23)

First lie: "My master has sent me." *Second lie:* "Two young men of the sons of the prophets have come" to stay, and money is needed for their lodging. *Third lie:* "My master has sent me, *saying* [emphasis added] . . ." He attributes the second lie to Elisha's lips. Gehazi returns to Elisha's house, where he covertly stashes the coins. Although not caught with his hands in the cookie jar, Gehazi has crumbs all over his red face.

> When he came to the hill, he took them from their hand
> and deposited them in the house, and he sent the men
> away, and they departed. But he went in and stood before
> his master. And Elisha said to him, "Where have you
> been, Gehazi?" And he said, "Your servant went nowhere."
> (vv. 24–25)

Fourth lie: "Your servant went nowhere."

We are often advised never to say never. But one never that seems appropriate is to never, never lie to a *prophet*. Of all the people in the world most likely to see through the scam and into the heart of things, it's a prophet! Listen to the penetrating questions that pierce through Gehazi's flimsy roof of lies. Then hear the scathing indictment.

> Then he said to him, "Did not my heart go with you, when the man turned from his chariot to meet you? Is it a time to receive money and to receive clothes and olive groves and vineyards and sheep and oxen and male and female servants? Therefore, the leprosy of Naaman shall cleave to you and to your descendants forever." So he went out from his presence a leper as white as snow. (vv. 26–27)

An Ironic Ending

Irony is a literary term that refers to a situation that is the tragic reverse of what is expected. Thus, it is ironic that King Arthur's Round Table was destroyed by Lancelot—the very man who helped build it. It is ironic that Eve expected great happiness eating the forbidden fruit when, in fact, it brought her great sorrow. It is ironic that Naaman, the Syrian, came away from Elisha *cleansed* while Gehazi, the Jew who lived as a servant in Elisha's own house, came away *cursed* (see Luke 4:27). It is ironic, too, that Naaman, the leper (2 Kings 5:1), became the servant (v. 18), and Gehazi, the servant (v. 20), became the leper (v. 27). In a downpour of poetic justice, Naaman's loose change became Gehazi's leprous curse. The truth about Gehazi leaked through his roof of thatched lies to expose his greed and drench it in God's sudden and torrential judgment.[3] If your life were made into a dramatic play, would the main character's flaws be visible—like Naaman's leprosy—or would they be hidden—like Gehazi's greed? Would the main character listen to the advice of servants—like Naaman—or would he be evasive to the words of his master—like Gehazi? Has your main character made a public profession of faith—like Naaman's washing in the Jordan—or is there a private world of hidden

---

3. Swift and certain judgment functions as a deterrent against evil (see Eccles. 8:11).

sin thatched with lies? These are questions you need to come to grips with—if you want your life to have a happy ending instead of a tragic one.

Living Insights

Study One

God used the lives of Naaman and Gehazi to paint a picture of contrasts. Let's look further into 2 Kings 5 to explore their differences.

- Copy the following chart into your notebook. As you read the twenty-seven verses of 2 Kings 5, jot down observations on both men. Put a check (√) in the appropriate column, signifying whether the trait was good or bad.

Naaman			Gehazi		
Observations	Good (√)	Bad (√)	Observations	Good (√)	Bad (√)

Living Insights

Study Two

"Because the sentence against an evil deed is not executed quickly, therefore the hearts of the sons of men among them are given fully to do evil" (Eccles. 8:11).

- Spend a few minutes meditating on this verse. It has a lot to say to us today. Why not commit this verse to memory? It will be time well spent.
- Are you, like Gehazi, guilty of deception? This is such a serious matter—please deal with it before the roof comes crashing down around you. It's so vital to clear your conscience before God, and perhaps also before the ones you've been deceiving: dads, moms, sons, daughters, employers, employees, neighbors, church friends . . . whomever. Remember, lies cover a multitude of sins—but only temporarily.

Jabez: Disabled
but Not Disqualified
1 Chronicles 4:9–10

Thousands of the world's best athletes compete in the Olympic Games. Each Olympian's body has been carefully sculpted, fine-tuned to guarantee optimum performance in the individual's event. Marathoners—slight, twig-like—must be able to endure a rapid pulse rate for more than twenty-six miles, so they spend their training time toning and expanding the heart. The swimmer's body—with its sturdy trunk—must be prepared to propel itself through the water, powerfully, forcefully, like a well-oiled machine. And the gymnasts—limber, catlike—must be swift enough to catch bars with their thighs . . . to complete the 2½ flip with a twist before reaching the floor. Every Olympian has what it takes to win. All are at their best, bearing no disabilities. But this is not the case in the game of life. The Old Testament gives us a prime example in Jabez, who was disabled but refused to let his handicap hamper his performance. He is an unknown competitor who appears on the scriptural playing field briefly and goes for the gold, never to be mentioned again. Jabez may not have made the "Hall of Faith" in Hebrews 11. His name may not even appear on a single game card in Bible Trivia. But his example—one of faith and fortitude—is challenging. His attitude, revolutionary.

I. A Glance at Jabez

If you blink, you'll miss it. But rising out of the dust of 1 Chronicles is a two-verse oasis where you catch a brief glimpse of a man who will whet your thirst for God.

> And Jabez was more honorable than his brothers, and his mother named him Jabez saying, "Because I bore him with pain." Now Jabez called on the God of Israel, saying, "Oh that Thou wouldst bless me indeed, and enlarge my border, and that Thy hand might be with me, and that Thou wouldst keep me from harm, that it may not pain me!" And God granted him what he requested.

A. His name (v. 9). His mother named him Jabez, which means "pain," "distress," or "vexation." The verse tells us that his mother "bore him with pain." This does not mean that she named him "pain" because she had a difficult delivery, but rather that his name reveals the times of hardship into which he was born. In other words, Jabez's family viewed him as salt in the open wounds of the days they lived in. We can't be certain as to exactly what kind of hardship or difficulty Jabez was born into. But we do know that he wore the tag "pain" his whole life.

B. His reputation (v. 9). Somehow, Jabez was able to rise above his situation, and he found himself distinguished and favorable among his brothers. The life of Jabez is proof that *incredible abilities often emerge from those with the least possibilities.* Jabez had to experience and endure pain before he could ultimately triumph over it.

> It will sometimes happen that where there is the most sorrow in the antecedents, there will be the most pleasure in the sequel. As the furious storm gives place to the clear sunshine, so the night of weeping precedes the morning of joy. Sorrow the harbinger; gladness the prince it ushers in.... More honourable than his brethren was the child whom his mother bore with sorrow.... The honour he enjoyed would not have been worth having if it had not been vigorously contested and equitably won.[1]

C. His faith (v. 10). From his prayer, we discover that Jabez was a believer. It isn't actually spelled out; it doesn't have to be. Instead of *telling* us about Jabez's faith, the writer *shows* us. We read, "Now Jabez called on the God of Israel." He offered a prayer of petition to God, for his hope was in the Lord.

Show or Tell?

How do others perceive your faith? Do they *listen* to your faith as you chat about it, sitting on the living room couch while you sip coffee? Or do they *see* it in your life, as you work, play, worship, love? "Little children, let us not love with word or with tongue, but in deed and truth" (1 John 3:18). While He was on earth, Jesus said, "Let your light shine before men in such a way that they may see your good works, and glorify your Father who is in heaven" (Matt. 5:16). You've heard the old adage, Actions speak louder than words. The Lord agrees. He wants us to bag the faith-talking and start faith-walking.

D. His prayer (v. 10). In his prayer—a prayer of motivation— Jabez asks four things of God.[2]

---

1. Charles H. Spurgeon, *The Treasury of the Bible* (Grand Rapids, Mich.: Zondervan Publishing House, 1968), vol. 2, p. 1.

2. One commentary gives some interesting information on the background of Jabez's prayer. "The prayer of his, ... which, like Jacob's, is in the form of a vow (Gen. 28:20), seems to have

Footnote continued on next page

1. **"Bless me indeed."** The last word of this prayer is the most significant. Jabez prays with God-sanctioned *vision,* asking God not merely to bless him, but to bless him *indeed.*[3] Like a true competitor, he wanted more than just to finish the race; he wanted to win.[4]

2. **"Enlarge my border."** With God-sanctioned *ambition,* Jabez asks God for increase. He was not content with either a usual blessing or with his present ministry. He refused to fill a little space; he wanted God to expand his opportunities for service.

> ## Personal Application
>
> Contentment. The Lord does want us to attain it (see Phil. 4:11b, 1 Tim. 6:6–8). But all too often we pat ourselves on the back, thinking that because we aren't complaining about our circumstances, we've found it. Actually, we are only wearing contentment to mask our laziness. There's a difference between an attitude that says "I'm fine right where I am" and one that says "I'm happy here, but does God have something more for me to do?" The former is passivity; the latter, true contentment. Have you settled for less than God's best in your life? Are you ignoring His tug to go somewhere, to be something—something that would challenge you? Are you shrugging it off, deluded by a sense of false contentment?

---

3. **"Thy hand might be with me."** Jabez was wise. He knew that if God enlarged his border, he would need even more

---

been uttered when he was entering on an important or critical service, for the successful execution of which he placed confidence neither on his own nor his people's prowess, but looked anxiously for the aid and blessing of God." Robert Jamieson, A. R. Fausset, and David Brown, *A Commentary on the Old and New Testaments* (Grand Rapids, Mich.: William B. Eerdmans Publishing Co., 1984), vol. 1, p. 459.

3. An excellent explanation of the "indeed blessing" is found in Spurgeon's sermon on 1 Chronicles 4:9–10. "There are many varieties of blessing. Some are blessings only in name: they gratify our wishes for a moment, but permanently disappoint our expectations. They charm the eye, but pall on the taste. Others are mere temporary blessings: they perish with the using. Though for awhile they regale the senses, they cannot satisfy the higher cravings of the soul. But, 'Oh that Thou wouldst bless me indeed!' . . . Let the grace of God prompt it, let the choice of God appoint it, let the bounty of God confer it, and then the endowment shall be something godlike indeed; something worthy of the lips that pronounce the benediction, and verily to be craved by every one who seeks honor that is substantial and enduring." Spurgeon, *Treasury of the Bible,* p. 1.

4. See 1 Corinthians 9:24, where Paul encourages us to run to win the prize.

to be led by His hand. With God-sanctioned *cooperation,* Jabez asks for God's guidance. He wasn't on a power trip. He asked for big blessings and big opportunities in ministry. And he was willing to humbly place his trust in a big God.

4. **"Keep me from harm, that it may not pain me!"** Finally, Jabez asks for God-sanctioned *protection.* In choosing to use the word *pain,* Jabez draws our attention to his name, which he links to his nature. He asks the Lord for protection—protection against himself and against the pattern that was so characteristic of him. It's as if Jabez is saying, "Let me not experience the grief which my name implies, and which my sins may well produce."[5] He prays that God would save him from his pessimistic past. Jabez was weary of his life of anguish. He wanted a fresh start, and he knew who to go to for help.

E. **His answer** (v. 10). The best part of this glimpse of Jabez is that "God granted him what he requested."[6] Everything he asked for, he received (compare Matt. 7:7, John 15:16, and James 4:2b). It's no wonder he was distinguished among his brothers.

II. A Glance at Ourselves

This short, crisp, historical sketch stimulates healthy self-evaluation. It raises three questions that everyone ought to answer.

A. **What is my name?** If God were to name you by your nature, what would He name you? Critical? Lazy? Seductive? Short-sighted? Sharp-tongued? Stubborn?

B. **Where am I spiritually?** Are you content to stay in your cozy, carpeted room—not wanting to get chilled by the outside air? Or are you willing to have your sphere of influence enlarged, to fill a big place for God?

C. **What am I asking of God?** Jabez asked big things of God, and he got them. This poem by Amy Carmichael displays Jabez's Olympic attitude.

> From prayer that asks that I may be
> Sheltered from winds that beat on Thee,
> From fearing when I should aspire,
> From faltering when I should climb higher,
> From silken self, O captain, free
> Thy soldier who would follow Thee.

5. Jamieson, Fausset, and Brown, *Commentary on the Old and New Testaments,* p. 459.

6. Unger's discussion of this prayer reminds us of the example of faith we see in Jabez's life. "God heard his faithful cry and answered his prayer, furnishing the centuries with an example of the faith in God and His redemptive grace that existed in the hearts of many Judahites." Merrill F. Unger, *Unger's Commentary on the Old Testament* (Chicago, Ill.: Moody Press, 1981), vol. 1, p. 543.

From subtle love of softening things,
From easy choices, weakenings,
Not thus are spirits fortified,
Not this way went the Crucified,
From all that dims Thy Calvary,
O Lamb of God, deliver me.

Give me the love that leads the way,
The faith that nothing can dismay,
The hope no disappointments tire,
The passion that will burn like fire,
Let me not sink to be a clod:
Make me Thy fuel, Flame of God.[7]

The Last Lap

An athlete has to be in perfect shape to compete in the Olympic Games, but there are also games for those whose bodies are far from perfect—the Special Olympics. In these games, the equipment for every event includes wheelchairs, leg braces, and catheters. Some contestants wear Nikes; some, shoes of two different sizes; others have no feet. But in the Special Olympics, all the participants have one thing in common—the courage to overcome. Face it— in some ways, like Jabez, we were all born handicapped. The question is, will you let your disabilities disqualify you, or will you get out on the track—with your heart, your faith, and your God?

Living Insights

Study One

Talk about getting started out on the wrong foot . . . how would you like to be given the name "Pain" at your birth? Names are rich in significance in the Scriptures. I'm sure you can think of many examples.

Continued on next page

---

7. Amy Carmichael, "Make Me Thy Fuel" in *Toward Jerusalem* (Fort Washington, Pa.: Christian Literature Crusade, 1961; London, England: Society for Promoting Christian Knowledge, 1950), p. 94.

- When we see a person's name in the Bible, it is often followed by a definition. It's fascinating to see how the name relates to the individual's personality. Choose some of the more familiar Bible characters, and fill in the following chart. You should be able to see the relationship between each name and the person it belongs to.

Names	Meanings	Relation between Names and Personalities

Living Insights

Study Two

Jabez is a striking contrast to the meaning of his name. In a sense, he overcame himself. How about you? Let's use this time for some introspection.

- What's your name? What word best describes your nature? Think back on what your personality has been like during the last six months, and jot down an answer or two.
- Let's expand this theme. Sit down with a pencil and paper, and sum up what has characterized your life during the last six months. What has been the major weakness in your life? Write it down.
- Now turn the paper over. What are you going to do about this weakness? Note your specific goals for overcoming it. Remember, it's important to get specific. How can you pursue God's will in this situation? Jot that down. Close with prayer, asking God for big things . . . expectantly.

Uzziah: The King Who Became a Leper

2 Chronicles 26

Tombstones—granite tongues of ashen gray—stand row after row in cemeteries like soldiers at attention. Epitaphs—chiseled testimonies of summarized lives—mutely face the sun . . . the rain . . . the wind . . . the snow, calling out to the generations that remain. Epitaphs can range anywhere from the trite to the tragic. They can vary in tone from the whimsical "I told you I was sick!" to the poetic:

> The body of
> Benjamin Franklin, printer,
> (Like the cover of an old book,
> Its contents worn out,
> And stript of its lettering and gilding)
> Lies here, food for worms!
> Yet the work itself shall not be lost,
> For it will, as he believed, appear once more,
> In a new
> And more beautiful edition,
> Corrected and amended
> By its Author![1]

As we enter the cemetery of Old Testament characters, we come across the grave of a man of great accomplishment: Uzziah, king of Israel. Suddenly, however, we are struck by an overwhelming incongruity. Where we would have expected a pyramid built as a memorial, we find only a small, simple grave marker. Where we would have expected an eloquent eulogy chiseled in stone, we read only these words etched on his marker: "He is a leper." How a man of Uzziah's monumental achievements came to be remembered so matter-of-factly, without feeling, without remorse, is the intriguing subject of our present study.

I. Uzziah as a Youth (2 Chronicles 26:1–5)

After Solomon's death, the reins of the kingdom fell into the hands of his son—the greedy, power-hungry Rehoboam. Holding tight reins on the ten northern tribes, headed by Jeroboam, he spurred them with sharp tax increases. Bucking his rule, the northern kingdom slipped out from underneath the binding saddle of his throne and seceded to form an independent nation. Consequently, Rehoboam was left to rule the two remaining tribes that he corralled to form the southern kingdom. The tenth king down the line from Rehoboam

---

1. Benjamin Franklin in *The Oxford Book of American Literary Anecdotes,* ed. Donald Hall (New York, N.Y.: Oxford University Press, 1981), p. 13.

was Uzziah, who ruled for fifty-two years, from 792–739 B.C. His was to be a path to prosperity—a path paved by parental influences.

> And all the people of Judah took Uzziah, who was sixteen years old, and made him king in the place of his father Amaziah. He built Eloth and restored it to Judah after the king slept with his fathers. Uzziah was sixteen years old when he became king, and he reigned fifty-two years in Jerusalem; and his mother's name was Jechiliah of Jerusalem. (vv. 1–3)

We learn from 2 Chronicles 25:2a that Uzziah's father "did right in the sight of the Lord." Undoubtedly, his father's example provided the pavement over which Uzziah was to walk. However, the second half of the verse unearths the sharp stone in the road over which Uzziah would one day fall: "yet not with a whole heart."

A Divided Heart

The clarion call trumpeted throughout the Old Testament and echoed in the New is:

> "You shall love the Lord your God with all your heart
> and with all your soul and with all your might."
> (Deut. 6:5)

The most sought-after territory on earth is not the oil fields of Saudi Arabia or the diamond mines of South Africa. It's your *heart.* Every past global war pales next to the white-hot battle being waged for your heart. For it, Satan gave up an eternity in heaven. For it, God gave up His only Son. If you love God, but not with your whole heart . . . if you serve God, but not with your whole heart, then a portion of your heart is unclaimed territory—up for grabs. And, if you surrender even an isolated, insignificant beachhead to Satan, he has a foothold that may someday give him the advantage he needs to overthrow your loyalty to the Lord. Won't you surrender to God and let Him plant His flag in *every* corner of your heart? A flag of the Lord's dominion over your life . . . to fly defiantly in the face of Satan . . . to fly colors unfurled so that others may see and rally behind it.

Following in his father's footsteps, Uzziah got off to a great start in his "Yellow Brick Road" to prosperity.

> And he did right in the sight of the Lord according to all that his father Amaziah had done. And he continued to seek God in the days of Zechariah, who had understanding through the vision of God; and as long as he sought the Lord, God prospered him. (vv. 4–5)

II. Uzziah as a Statesman (2 Chronicles 26:6–15)

The bricks to Uzziah's prosperity were gilded by the golden touch of God's blessing.

> Now he went out and warred against the Philistines, and broke down the wall of Gath and the wall of Jebneh and the wall of Ashdod; and he built cities in the area of Ashdod and among the Philistines. And God helped him against the Philistines, and against the Arabians who lived in Gur-baal, and the Meunites. The Ammonites also gave tribute to Uzziah, and his fame extended to the border of Egypt, for he became very strong. Moreover, Uzziah built towers in Jerusalem at the Corner Gate and at the Valley Gate and at the corner buttress and fortified them. And he built towers in the wilderness and hewed many cisterns, for he had much livestock, both in the lowland and in the plain. He also had plowmen and vinedressers in the hill country and the fertile fields, for he loved the soil. Moreover, Uzziah had an army ready for battle, which entered combat by divisions, according to the number of their muster, prepared by Jeiel the scribe and Maaseiah the official, under the direction of Hananiah, one of the king's officers. The total number of the heads of the households, of valiant warriors, was 2,600. And under their direction was an elite army of 307,500, who could wage war with great power, to help the king against the enemy. Moreover, Uzziah prepared for all the army shields, spears, helmets, body armor, bows and sling stones. And in Jerusalem he made engines of war invented by skillful men to be on the towers and on the corners, for the purpose of shooting arrows and great stones. Hence his fame spread afar, for he was marvelously helped until he was strong. (vv. 6–15)

Politically, Uzziah's leadership resulted in triumph over his enemies (vv. 6–8) and great accomplishments in his kingdom (vv. 9–10). *Militarily,* he was organized, prepared (vv. 11–14), and inventive (v. 15). *Personally,* "his fame extended to the border of Egypt, for he became very strong" (v. 8b, see also v. 15b).

The Blurred Hand of Blessing

Prosperity followed Uzziah as long as he sought the Lord (26:5). Throughout the Old Testament we are exhorted to seek the Lord (Pss. 9:10, 22:26, 24:6, 34:10, 70:4, 105:3), recognizing Him as our refuge, our strength, and our source of blessing. However, once prosperity comes, it's easy to focus so intently on blessing in the foreground that His hand in the background—

---

from which the blessing comes—is blurred. When that happens, the only hand we see in the picture is ours, thus preparing the way for pride. God's warning to the Israelites before they enter into the blessings of the Promised Land serves to correct our vision.

> "Beware lest you forget the Lord your God . . . lest, when you have eaten and are satisfied . . . and when your herds and your flocks multiply, and your silver and gold multiply, and all that you have multiplies, then your heart becomes proud, and you forget the Lord your God who brought you out from the land of Egypt, out of the house of slavery. He led you through the great and terrible wilderness, with its fiery serpents and scorpions and thirsty ground where there was no water; He brought water for you out of the rock of flint. In the wilderness He fed you manna which your fathers did not know, that He might humble you and that He might test you, to do good for you in the end. Otherwise, you may say in your heart, 'My power and the strength of my hand made me this wealth.' But you shall remember the Lord your God, for it is He who is giving you power to make wealth. . . . " (Deut. 8:11–18a)

Look around at your blessings—family, health, friends, home, job, material possessions. Whose hand do you see providing them? If you have to squint to see God's hand, maybe you're the one who has blurred the picture. Remember: "In Him we live and move and exist" (Acts 17:28). Conversely, *without Him,* we would be able to do nothing. Therefore, *to Him,* and Him alone, should go the glory and praise.

III. Uzziah as a Rebel (2 Chronicles 26:16–18)

Tragically, Uzziah believed his own press clippings. We read: "His fame extended to the border of Egypt, for he became *very strong"* (v. 8b, emphasis added). Again, in verse 15b: "Hence his fame spread afar, for he was marvelously helped until he was *strong"* (emphasis added). As he skipped footloose through poppy fields of his own pride, Uzziah lost consciousness of the God who had helped him prosper.

> But when he became strong, his heart was so proud that he acted corruptly, and he was unfaithful to the Lord his God, for he entered the temple of the Lord to burn incense on the altar of incense. Then Azariah the priest entered after him and with him eighty priests of the Lord, valiant

men. And they opposed Uzziah the king and said to him, "It is not for you, Uzziah, to burn incense to the Lord, but for the priests, the sons of Aaron who are consecrated to burn incense. Get out of the sanctuary, for you have been unfaithful, and will have no honor from the Lord God." (vv. 16–18)

A Quote to Consider

In his book *Mere Christianity,* C. S. Lewis discusses man's greatest sin—pride.

The essential vice, the utmost evil, is Pride. Unchastity, anger, greed, drunkenness, and all that, are mere fleabites in comparison: it was through Pride that the devil became the devil: Pride leads to every other vice: it is the complete anti-God state of mind.... As long as you are proud you cannot know God. A proud man is always looking down on things and people: and, of course, as long as you are looking down, you cannot see something that is above you.[2]

IV. Uzziah as a Leper (2 Chronicles 26:19–23)

Preening over his strength, Uzziah believed himself to be bigger than life, thus totally crowding God out of the scene. And like a narcissistic movie star with an inflated ego, Uzziah was vulnerably poised for the critic's pinprick.

But Uzziah, with a censer in his hand for burning incense, was enraged; and while he was enraged with the priests, the leprosy broke out on his forehead before the priests in the house of the Lord, beside the altar of incense. And Azariah the chief priest and all the priests looked at him, and behold, he was leprous on his forehead; and they hurried him out of there, and he himself also hastened to get out because the Lord had smitten him. And King Uzziah was a leper to the day of his death; and he lived in a separate house, being a leper, for he was cut off from the house of the Lord. And Jotham his son was over the king's house judging the people of the land. Now the rest of the acts of Uzziah, first to last, the prophet Isaiah, the son of Amoz, has written. So Uzziah slept with his fathers, and they buried him with his fathers in the field of the

---

2. *A Mind Awake: An Anthology of C. S. Lewis,* ed. Clyde S. Kilby (New York, N.Y.: Harcourt, Brace and World, 1969), p. 115.

grave which belonged to the kings, for they said, "He is a leper." And Jotham his son became king in his place.

─── *A Closing Epitaph* ───────────────────────────
The words "He is a leper" are chiseled into the cold granite memory of Scripture as a tragic epitaph to one whose fame once reached the very borders of the mighty Egyptian empire. Hawthorne was correct when he said: "A grave, wherever it is found, preaches a short and pithy sermon to the soul."[3] If you died today, what words would etch your tombstone? What sermon would those words preach about your life?

Living Insights

Study One ■━━━━━━━━━━━━━━━━━━━━━━━━━━━━━

Perhaps no test is more demanding than success. The life story of King Uzziah testifies to this fact. It's important to *personalize* a story like this one; paraphrasing will help.

● Reread 2 Chronicles 26:1–23. When you feel that you understand it, write out the story in your own words. This technique is called paraphrasing, and it helps you to experience the thoughts and feelings of these biblical characters. Significant truths should surface as a result of this study. Whether you feel like a success or a failure, there is something from Uzziah's life you can learn.

Living Insights

Study Two ■━━━━━━━━━━━━━━━━━━━━━━━━━━━━━

Some very practical theology surfaces in this study—not the least of which is learning to deal with *success*. You might think, "I'd give anything just to have success! Don't worry, I'll deal with it!" These are often famous last words. Let's discuss the following observations.

● *No genuine success is possible apart from the Lord.* Do you agree with this principle? How do you explain those ungodly people around you who seem outwardly successful? Is there a formula for success? If so, what is it? If not, why not?

● *There are few tests like the one success brings.* Why? Have you personally been put to this test? If so, share how you handled it. Do you know others put to this test? How did they handle it?

───
3. Nathaniel Hawthorne in *1,001 Sermon Illustrations and Quotations,* comp. Geikie, Cowper, et al. (Grand Rapids, Mich.: Baker Book House, 1954), p. 54.

- *The Lord who blesses us is also able to bruise and break us.* Can you back up this principle with Scriptures? Share them. Why would God want to bruise or break us? Where are you in this whole process?

From Captive to Queen:
An Adoption Story

Romans 8, Galatians 4, Esther

Most of us haven't had to look abortion in the eyes. We read about it, shudder at the thought of it, even campaign against it. But we never really get close enough to see its blackness. Only the few who enclose themselves within the cold, clean walls to watch the act . . . only they understand what really happens. One surgeon, a pro-life advocate, poignantly expresses his reaction to witnessing an abortion.

> I know. We cannot feed the great numbers. There is no more room. I know, I know. It is a woman's right to refuse the risk, to decline the pain of childbirth. And an unwanted child is a very great burden. An unwanted child is a burden to himself. I know.
>
> And yet . . . there is the flick of that needle. I *saw* it. I saw . . . I *felt*—in that room, a pace away, life prodded, life fending off. I saw life avulsed—swept by flood, blackening—then *out*.
>
> There, says the doctor. It's all over. It wasn't too bad, was it? he says to the woman.
>
> She smiles. It is all over. Oh, yes.
>
> And who would care to imagine that from a moist and dark commencement six months before there would ripen the cluster and globule, the sprout and pouch of man?[1]

The purpose of this lesson is not to dwell on the atrocity of abortion, the cruelty of man—the dark side. Rather, it is to radiate the alternative—the light and warmth of adoption. It extends the hand of salvation to all involved. When an adoptive couple finally holds a child in their arms—their child—they are saved from the anxiety of waiting, or the anguish of infertility. It's as if the living, breathing bundle instantly soothes their pain. And the child is saved too—perhaps from being unwanted, or raised by incompetent parents, or thoughtlessly snuffed out. Adoption is God's candle in the black abysses of childlessness and abortion. In this lesson we will see how God used Esther's adoption to raise her status from an orphaned captive to a beloved queen. Likewise, we will learn how we have been lifted from hell's pit to be joint heirs with the King.

I. The Theology of Adoption (Romans 8, Galatians 4)

Romans 8 is the *magnum opus,* the *sine qua non* of Paul's theological statement about life with God. Specifically, Paul talks about some of the benefits of being connected with God's family (vv. 1–15). First, we are protected *forever* from God's condemnation (v. 1). Second, we are set free from the oppressive bondage of sin and death (v. 2).

1. Richard Selzer, *Mortal Lessons* (New York, N.Y.: Simon and Schuster, 1976), pp. 159–60.

54

Third, we receive the power of the Holy Spirit, which enables us to spurn the flesh and walk "according to the Spirit" (v. 4). Fourth, we gain the mind of the Spirit, which is "life and peace" (v. 6). Fifth, we have the righteousness of God (v. 10). Sixth, we have assurance that we will be resurrected from the dead (v. 13). Galatians 4 underscores these rich truths about adoption:

> God sent forth His Son, born of a woman, born under the Law, in order that He might redeem those who were under the Law, that we might receive the adoption[2] as sons. (vv. 4b–5)

In other words, God reaches into the slave market of sin, breaks our fetters, and redeems[3] us as we come to Him by faith. We are no longer slaves, but sons and heirs through God (v. 7); we are entitled to a wealth of privileges and responsibilities.

A Christmas Gift with an Easter Bow

Many of us who have accepted God's offer of salvation are still trying to find a way to pay Him back. We come to God with one hand extended, and the other groping around in our front pocket for loose change. It's our instinct to want to pay our debts—to even things up. After all, we've got to be responsible. Have you let the "if anyone will not work, neither let him eat" (2 Thess. 3:10b) principle infect your theology? Do you think that the more church committees you belong to, Sunday school classes you teach, Third World children you sponsor, the more worthy you'll be of God's gift of eternal life? The gift *did* come at a great price—God's only begotten Son. But to us, it comes free—without strings or buy now, pay later conditions. It's been paid for ... *totally* ... by Jesus.

II. A Biography of Adoption (Esther)

Biographically, the Book of Esther illustrates the theological truth of adoption. Esther was a young Jewish woman who was orphaned, then mercifully adopted by her cousin Mordecai (2:5–7). This drama

---

2. The term *adoption* is a rich one. It comes from a combination of two Greek words: *huios,* meaning "son," and *tithēmi,* which means "to sit, to place, to put." The result is the term *huiothesia,* which means "the placement of a son." For more references to adoption, see Romans 9:4 and Ephesians 1:5.

3. The Greek word for *redemption* is used of the price of redeeming something that is in pawn, of the money paid to ransom prisoners of war, and of money paid to buy a slave's freedom. Titus 2:13b–14 lists the price of our salvation: " ... our great God and Savior, Christ Jesus; who gave *Himself* for us" (emphasis added). For more references on redemption, see Mark 10:45, 1 Timothy 2:6, and Romans 3:24. Also see *The Apostolic Preaching of the Cross,* by Leon Morris (Grand Rapids, Mich.: William B. Eerdmans Publishing Co., 1960), pp. 9–59.

stars three more characters: Ahasuerus, king of Persia, also known as Xerxes; Vashti, the king's beautiful wife; and Haman, the one who wears the black hat. Out of the sixty-six books in the Bible, Esther is the only one that doesn't mention the name of God. But even though His name is absent, His providential fingerprints can be found throughout. Replete with action and intrigue, this ancient story of adoption still speaks to us.

A Hushed Note

Too often, if God's name isn't billboarded in front of us, we can't see Him . . . can't feel the warmth of His breath. But God doesn't always advertise His presence. Sometimes, He only whispers it. He wants us to be sensitive to His subtle ways. Just as Adam and Eve heard the sound of God walking in the garden (Gen. 3:8), we also need to put our ears to the ground and listen for the silent thunder of His gentle footsteps as He sovereignly walks the earth.

A. **A feast marked by punishment** (1:1–22). King Ahasuerus threw a big bash for the entire populace of Susa, the capital city of the Persian Empire (v. 5). During the seven days of this revelry, "the royal wine was plentiful according to the king's bounty" (v. 7). On the seventh day, when "the king was merry with wine," he decided to send for Queen Vashti to come in and parade her beauty in front of his guests (vv. 10–11). But Vashti said no, which in her day was not a popular thing to do. Many modern women would have applauded Vashti's liberated conduct, but not King Ahasuerus. He was so angry, his wrath burned so within him, that he sought counsel on what disciplinary measures he should take with Vashti (vv. 12–15). Concerned that the queen's rebelliousness would license the other married women in the Persian kingdom to disobey their husbands, the king was advised to ban her from his presence and replace her with a more deserving woman.

B. **An ancient beauty contest** (2:1–20). To find Vashti's replacement, the king staged a beauty pageant. The entire kingdom was scoured so he could choose the most beautiful young virgin. Mordecai entered Esther in the contest, advising her not to reveal her Jewish background. And as the finger of God began to move through the streets of Susa, it landed sovereignly on Esther.

> And the king loved Esther more than all the women,
> and she found favor and kindness with him more
> than all the virgins, so that he set the royal crown
> on her head and made her queen instead of Vashti.
> (v. 17)

C. A crucial subplot (2:21–23). After this climactic scene, the camera seems to wander inadvertently to an extraneous subplot. In this Alfred Hitchcock scene, Mordecai learns of a plot to assassinate the king and reports it to Esther, who then informs the king "in Mordecai's name" (v. 22). After a thorough investigation, Mordecai's information was verified, the two conspirators were hung, and "it was written in the Book of the Chronicles in the king's presence" (v. 23). Tuck this scene away in your mind until later. After seeing God's sovereign hand, we will understand its significance.

D. A promotion and a plot (3:1–15). Meanwhile, Haman is promoted to the king's right-hand man, and the king commanded everyone to pay homage to Haman. But Mordecai, aware of Haman's greed and conceit, "neither bowed down nor paid homage" (v. 2b). And he was not about to be excused from such disobedience.

> When Haman saw that Mordecai neither bowed down nor paid homage to him, Haman was filled with rage. But he disdained to lay hands on Mordecai alone, for they had told him who the people of Mordecai were; therefore Haman sought to destroy all the Jews, the people of Mordecai, who were throughout the whole kingdom of Ahasuerus. (vv. 5–6)

An ancient Holocaust took shape in the mind of this Old Testament Hitler. In verses 8 and 9, Haman unveils his plot to the king.

> Then Haman said to King Ahasuerus, "There is a certain people scattered and dispersed among the peoples in all the provinces of your kingdom; their laws are different from those of all other people, and they do not observe the king's laws, so it is not in the king's interest to let them remain. If it is pleasing to the king, let it be decreed that they be destroyed, and I will pay ten thousand talents of silver into the hands of those who carry on the king's business, to put into the king's treasuries."

The king's response undoubtedly made Haman grin:

> Then the king took his signet ring from his hand and gave it to Haman, . . . the enemy of the Jews. And the king said to Haman, "The silver is yours, and the people also, to do with them as you please." (vv. 10–11)

E. A creative plan (4:1–5:14). After discovering Haman's plot, Mordecai gets the word to Esther.

> Then Mordecai told them to reply to Esther, "Do not imagine that you in the king's palace can escape any more than all the Jews. For if you remain silent at this

time, relief and deliverance will arise for the Jews from another place and you and your father's house will perish. And who knows whether you have not attained royalty for such a time as this?" (vv. 13–14)

Talk about great rhetoric! It's as if Mordecai is saying, "This is your meeting with destiny, Esther. This is why God had me take you as a little girl and rear you His way. This is God's work. Don't be silent. Speak up!" And Esther gave this reply to Mordecai:

"Go, assemble all the Jews who are found in Susa, and fast for me; do not eat or drink for three days, night or day. I and my maidens also will fast in the same way. And thus I will go in to the king, which is not according to the law; and if I perish, I perish." (v. 16)

Risking her life, Esther comes before the king without a summons. He openly welcomes her into his presence and beckons her to make her request. She puts the king off momentarily, inviting him and Haman to a banquet she had prepared. While dining together, she invites them to a banquet on the next day, when she promises to reveal her request (5:1–8). Pleased with being considered part of the royalty, his head swelling with pride, Haman leaves the feast. However, his good feelings are squelched at the sight of Mordecai, who still refuses to bow down to him. Enraged, Haman plots to have Mordecai hanged the next morning (5:9–14).

A Close-up of Esther

On the old metal scale that measures faith against works, Esther weighs in evenly. Notice her well-balanced response to Mordecai's plea. Notice how she asks the Jews to fast with her for three days, to display externally the seriousness of their prayers to God—stacking the weight on the works side. Notice also her words, "If I perish, I perish" (4:16), which demonstrate her firm confidence in God's plan—adding weight to the faith side. It's true. God's gift of salvation is free—received by faith alone. But our works are its vital signs, proof that our faith is alive and active (see James 2:17–18). Take a look at the New Testament scale in perfect balance:

For by grace you have been saved through faith; and that not of yourselves, *it is the gift of God; not as a result of works,* that no one should boast. For we are His workmanship, *created in Christ Jesus for good works,* which God prepared beforehand, that we should walk in them. (Eph. 2:8–10, emphasis added)

> Is the faith pan of your spiritual scale scraping the tabletop while the works pan hangs elevated and empty? Or is your scale tipped toward the works tray, leaving the faith tray sorely wanting?

F. A reading of remembrance and overdue honor (6:1–14). That night, while the gallows were being built, King Ahasuerus couldn't sleep, "so he gave an order to bring the book of records, the chronicles, and they were read before the king" (v. 1). Reminded that Mordecai had tipped him off about the conspiracy, King Ahasuerus decides to honor him. So the king sends for Haman and asks, "What is to be done for the man whom the king desires to honor?" (v. 6). Certain that the king wanted to honor *him,* Haman answers:

> "For the man whom the king desires to honor, let them bring a royal robe which the king has worn, and the horse on which the king has ridden, and on whose head a royal crown has been placed; and let the robe and the horse be handed over to one of the king's most noble princes and let them array the man whom the king desires to honor and lead him on horseback through the city square, and proclaim before him, 'Thus it shall be done to the man whom the king desires to honor.' " (vv. 7–9)[4]

The king takes this advice. But to Haman's shame, *he* has to honor Mordecai. What dramatic irony! After carrying out the king's wishes, Haman "hurried home, mourning, with his head covered" (v. 12).

G. Exposure and justice (7:1–10:3). That evening, at Esther's banquet, the king again asks Esther to reveal her request.

> Then Queen Esther answered and said, "If I have found favor in your sight, O king, and if it please the king, let my life be given me as my petition, and my people as my request; for we have been sold, I and my people, to be destroyed, to be killed and to be annihilated. Now if we had only been sold as slaves, men and women, I would have remained silent, for

---

4. Theologian Merrill Unger makes an interesting comment on Haman's pride. "What an illustration of the truth that 'pride goeth before destruction, and an haughty spirit before a fall' (Prov. 16:18; cf. 18:12). The honors Haman's pride would bestow upon himself were to be bestowed upon his enemy, Mordecai, the Jew, hatred for whom had deprived him of all sense and reason, and like all his ilk, made him a colossal megalomaniac." Merrill F. Unger, *Unger's Commentary on the Old Testament* (Chicago, Ill.: Moody Press, 1981), vol. 1, p. 665.

the trouble would not be commensurate with the annoyance to the king." (7:3–4)

The king asks Esther, "Who is he, and where is he, who would presume to do thus?" (v. 5). Esther responds, "A foe and an enemy, is this wicked Haman!" (v. 6). The king, outraged, had Haman hung on the very gallows he had built to execute Mordecai. Haman's plot to destroy the Jews was foiled because of Esther's courage—an adopted woman who risked her life to save her people. The book closes with the Feast of Purim ("Peace"), which is still celebrated by the Jews in Esther's honor (8:1–10:3).

III. The Practicality of Adoption

Esther's story illustrates not only the beauty of spiritual adoption but of physical adoption as well. Remembering these three truths will help us sight the unique significance of adoption.

A. The adoption process best models the way people enter God's family. Families with adopted children are living illustrations of salvation. Like adoptive parents, who reach into humanity and *choose* a child, and not on the child's merit, God has mercifully reached out and said, "You're unique, and you're Mine."

B. Adopted children often become God's special instruments. Like He did with Esther, God sometimes chooses adopted children to fulfill His special purposes. Their destinies have been changed; many have been preserved, rescued from dire circumstances to fulfill God's purposes in the light of His love.

C. People who are touched by the adopted realize how profound God's plan is. If you've brushed lives with adopted children, you understand the graciousness of God's redemptive design.

Chosen to Live

Throughout the story of Esther, we see so clearly God's sovereign plan of salvation. With hindsight, we can see His hand in each detail of the story. Separately, each detail is a disjointed pearl. But God took this pile of pearls, strung them together, and added a clasp to create something beautiful and useful. Like an adopted child—who was not aborted but allowed to live—our destinies were altered when we became part of God's family. The individual pearls of our lives have been threaded together to form a life of purpose and meaning. We have been saved from the death we were headed for and have been chosen instead to live.

Living Insights

The story of Queen Esther is a fascinating one. Even though it may be in one of the dustier portions of your Bible, this dramatic account is rich in truth.

● Imagine you are a cub reporter for the *Persian Post.* Your first assignment is to cover the story of the captive who became a queen. Read through Esther 1–7. The following chart will help you ask all the questions you'll need to write your article. Be sure to get all the facts—we want to keep you on at this newspaper!

| From Captive to Queen: Esther 1–7 ||
Questions	Answers
Who?	
What?	
Where?	
When?	
Why?	
How?	

Living Insights

People have many different thoughts and feelings about adoption. Some people are excited about being adopted; others seem to pity children who are adopted. How do you feel about it? Let's see.

● What are the similarities between natural birth and adoption?
● What are the differences?
● What advantages do adopted people enjoy?
● What disadvantages do they live with?
● Do you treat adopted children differently? Why or why not?
● How do you treat couples who want to adopt?
● What can you learn from the theology of spiritual adoption to help you understand and appreciate adoption in the physical realm?

Mr. Jones, Meet Mr. Jonah
Jonah

Written in 1851 by Herman Melville, *Moby Dick* breaches the sea of world literature to surface as an international classic. In chapter 9, one of Melville's characters, Father Mapple, begins a sermon on the Book of Jonah.

"Shipmates, this book, containing only four chapters—four yarns—is one of the smallest strands in the mighty cable of the Scriptures. Yet what depths of the soul does Jonah's deep sea-line sound! what a pregnant lesson to us is this prophet! What a noble thing is that canticle in the fish's belly! How billow-like and boisterously grand! We feel the floods surging over us; we sound with him to the kelpy bottom of the waters; seaweed and all the slime of the sea is about us! But *what* is this lesson that the book of Jonah teaches?"[1]

As we set sail on our voyage into Jonah, we are captivated by the story's high-seas drama. At the same time, our lives are plumbed by its emotion and anchored by its application. Though a whale dominates our thoughts of Jonah, like *Moby Dick,* it is a story not about a whale but about man, nature, and God. Before we loosen our moorings to embark onto the open seas, let's load a few pieces of introductory cargo.

I. Was Jonah Fictional or Factual?

The first crate we must take aboard is this weighty issue: Did a man by the name of Jonah actually live? Second Kings 14:23–25 answers the question, nailing down Jonah's name in history.

> In the fifteenth year of Amaziah the son of Joash king of Judah, Jeroboam the son of Joash king of Israel became king in Samaria, and reigned forty-one years. And he did evil in the sight of the Lord; he did not depart from all the sins of Jeroboam the son of Nebat, which he made Israel sin. He restored the border of Israel from the entrance of Hamath as far as the Sea of the Arabah, according to the word of the Lord, the God of Israel, which He spoke through His servant Jonah the son of Amittai, the prophet, who was of Gath-hepher.

We know that Jeroboam was a real king, that Hamath and the Sea of the Arabah were real places, and that Israel was a real nation. Therefore, it is logical to assume that Jonah, too, was a real person. Critics, however, might respond by saying that this reference concerned another prophet named Jonah, not the one depicted in the Book of Jonah. But, if we compare 2 Kings 14:25 with Jonah 1:1–2, the

---

1. Herman Melville, *Moby Dick; or, The Whale,* in vol. 48 of *Great Books of the Western World,* ed. Robert Maynard Hutchins (Chicago, Ill.: Encyclopaedia Britannica, 1971), p. 31.

descriptions appear identical. Both men are prophets, both are named Jonah, and both are referred to as the "son of Amittai." Another passage substantiating the historicity of Jonah is Matthew 12:38–41.

> Then some of the scribes and Pharisees answered Him, saying, "Teacher, we want to see a sign from You." But He answered and said to them, "An evil and adulterous generation craves for a sign; and yet no sign shall be given to it but the sign of Jonah the prophet; for just as Jonah was three days and three nights in the belly of the sea monster, so shall the Son of Man be three days and three nights in the heart of the earth. The men of Nineveh shall stand up with this generation at the judgment, and shall condemn it because they repented at the preaching of Jonah; and behold, something greater than Jonah is here."

Here our Lord connects a man named Jonah to a real city, Nineveh, as well as to an actual event, His Resurrection. Had Jonah been a mythological character, it is doubtful Jesus would have linked him, even literarily, to so crucial an event as the Resurrection. Jesus called Jonah a prophet (v. 39), mentioned his days in the large fish's belly (v. 40), and noted his preaching (v. 41). Both 2 Kings and Christ's testimony affirm the authenticity of Jonah. Consequently, we sail in well-charted seas when we hoist the historical flag over Jonah's name.

II. How Are We to Understand the Book?

Turning our attention from the person of Jonah to the Book of Jonah[2] is like turning our faces to the biting winds of a severe storm. No book in the Bible has been as badly battered by a sea of criticism as Jonah. Some people believe the book is a parable—an earthly story with a heavenly meaning—similar to the story of the Prodigal Son (Luke 15:11–32). But this view disregards the fact that Christ, in the same book (11:29–30), regards Jonah as a historical person. Some see the book as allegory, like John Bunyan's *Pilgrim's Progress,* where the story's true meaning can only be found by translating its characters and events into the truths they symbolize. Jonah's narrative, however, lacks the obvious allegorical signposts of *Pilgrim's Progress,* where Christian encounters such characters as Great Despair and Mr. Worldly Wiseman on his journey to the Celestial City. In Jonah, all the signs are posted along real routes traveled by real people on their way to real cities. The final interpretative option is to accept

---

2. Scholars have argued from Jonah 1:1 that the book never states it is Jonah's autobiography. But the autobiographical accounts of Hosea, Joel, Micah, Zephaniah, Haggai, Zechariah, and Malachi begin in a similar way.

the book at face value—as a historical narrative.[3] The traditional explanation has been questioned in modern times due to the miraculous nature of the book's events. Consequently, if you reject the miraculous from the outset, you have to reject the book's historical character as well. But, if you accept the miraculous intervention of God in human events, then accepting the book as a straightforward historical account should pose no problem. Certainly, if you accept the miracle of the fish and loaves, then the miracle of the fish and Jonah shouldn't be too hard to swallow! To understand the book's message, we need to cast a net that catches the essentials and allows the incidentals to slip away. The message is not the story of a man swallowed by a fish. It is an account of how God dealt with a reluctant and recalcitrant prophet who stubbornly refused to obey Him by carrying His Word to Israel's enemy. When we draw the net tighter, these incidental fingerlings slip back into the water: the ship . . . the sea . . . the fish . . . the dry land . . . the plant . . . the worm. The story of Jonah becomes evident when we divide it into four parts. In chapter 1, he's running *from* God; in chapter 2, he's running *to* God; in chapter 3, he's running *with* God; in chapter 4, he's running *against* God.

Last Call: All Aboard!

Before we get out of the harbor, may I ask you to take an honest look at your itinerary? Are you sailing on the wrong boat? Headed in the wrong direction? Stowing away with Jonah? Maybe not completely—but there may be an area where you're reluctant to follow the Lord. Are you running from a command in His Word—one that's difficult to obey? If so, it's time to get it on deck and out in the open. Confess it to God . . . before your ship heads into what will certainly be stormy weather.

III. Why Didn't Jonah Want to Go to Nineveh?

What would cause God's prophet to flee from His presence? Most commentators list three reasons: fear, prejudice, and pride. Some say Jonah feared stepping into enemy land. This is doubtful because he was not afraid to board the ship—there is no word that he feared the storm, no hint that he feared dying at sea. Others say that since Jonah was a Jew, he didn't want to lower himself to take a message

---

3. The historical places referred to are Nineveh (1:2), Tarshish, and Joppa (v. 3). Furthermore, the population of Nineveh, approximated by some scholars to be 600,000 (based on a population of 120,000 persons in 4:11), is substantiated by archaeological evidence. See *The Biblical World: A Dictionary of Biblical Archaeology,* ed. Charles F. Pfeiffer (Grand Rapids, Mich.: Baker Book House, 1966), pp. 415–17.

from God to the Gentiles. While on board, however, he expressed a deep compassion for the welfare of the idol-worshiping sailors, telling them to toss him overboard if they wanted to stop the storm. Still others say pride kept Jonah from going to Nineveh. If he went declaring a message of judgment and the people repented, God would show mercy, and Jonah's prophecy would be null and void. His credentials as a prophet in Jeroboam's court would be greatly devalued if not bankrupt altogether. Why didn't Jonah want to go to Nineveh? The answer is found in chapter 4, verse 2. Jonah clearly states that he fled to Tarshish because he knew God would show the Ninevites mercy if they repented.

"Therefore, in order to forestall this I fled to Tarshish, for
I knew that Thou art a gracious and compassionate God,
slow to anger and abundant in lovingkindness, and one
who relents concerning calamity."

Their cup of wickedness was full ... their days were numbered ... their doom was certain. This was fine with Jonah, as Nineveh was a mistress kingdom to the powerful empire of Assyria, Israel's arch-enemy.[4] Assyria was a brutal foe, a barbarous people with a horrible mania for blood and vengeance. It is no wonder that Jonah wanted them destroyed.

IV. Did a Whale Actually Swallow Jonah?

The next bit of introductory baggage deals with the whale in our tale. First, the text says the whale was "appointed" by God (1:17). The term is never used in the sense of creating but of *assigning* or *ordaining*.[5] Second, note that the phrase "great fish" was used instead of the word *whale*.[6] What's in view here is probably a whale shark, which grows to enormous proportions and is not, by nature, a man-eater. But could an enormous fish—whale or otherwise—really swallow a whole man? In his commentary on Jonah, C. F. Keil notes one such instance with a shark and a sailor.[7] Interpreting the

---

4. Nineveh, the capital of Assyria since the time of Sennacherib, embodied human self-exaltation. Brutal in warfare, barbaric in the slaughter of his captives, Sennacherib called himself "the great king" (2 Kings 18:28) and arrogantly thought of himself as a self-made military genius in his program of world conquest (Isa. 10:12–14). These are the associations that probably came to Jonah's mind when he thought of Nineveh. Jonah undoubtedly shared Nahum's sentiments about Nineveh's downfall in 612 B.C. "Woe to the bloody city, completely full of lies and pillage.... 'Nineveh is devastated!/Who will grieve for her?'...All who hear about you/Will clap their hands over you,...For on whom has not your evil passed continually?" (Nahum 3:1, 7, and 19).

5. The Hebrew term is *manah.*

6. The Hebrew term *dag gadol* literally means "great fish." In the New Testament, this term is translated *kētos,* meaning "sea monster" (see Matt. 12:40).

7. C. F. Keil, *Minor Prophets,* vol. 10 of *Commentary on the Old Testament in Ten Volumes* (Grand Rapids, Mich.: William B. Eerdmans Publishing Co., n.d.), p. 398.

"great fish" of Jonah 1:17 to possibly mean a whale, R. K. Harrison notes several reported cases of whales swallowing men alive.

As regards the credibility of the event described, it has frequently been remarked that the true whale has such a narrow gullet that it could only swallow comparatively small fish, and certainly nothing approaching the size of a man. In this general connection, however, it is important to observe that the Hebrew spoke of a "great fish" (Jon. 1:17), that is to say, some kind of sea denizen, and that the interpretation "whale" is the result of translations into English. Furthermore, while the true whale, whose habitat is the Arctic Ocean rather than the Mediterranean Sea, cannot swallow a man, the sperm whale or *cachalot* most probably can. Despite this constitutional obstacle it was shown as long ago as 1915 that even a true whale could save a man from drowning if he managed to negotiate the air-supply tract of the mammal and reach the great laryngeal pouch.... On another occasion a whale-hunter was reportedly swallowed in 1891, but was recovered the following day in unconscious condition from the inside of the mammal. Again, a seaman was said to have been swallowed by a large sperm whale in the vicinity of the Falkland Islands, and after three days was recovered unconscious but alive, though with some damage to his skin.[8]

Moby Dick—Maybe Shark . . . Maybe You

Whether the "great fish" was a whale, a whale shark, or some other sea creature, the great miracle of Jonah was not that he was swallowed or that he was kept alive for three days. The miracle was the Ninevites' response to the message Jonah preached. One and all, great and small, they repented and transferred their allegiance to the one true "Great King"—the Lord of hosts. A miracle like that can happen in your life— right now—as you read this. God can touch your heart, and with His compassion, change your life as He changed the lives of the Ninevites.

---

8. Roland Kenneth Harrison, *Introduction to the Old Testament* (Grand Rapids, Mich.: William B. Eerdmans Publishing Co., 1969), p. 907, as originally quoted from the following sources: G. Macloskie, *Bibliotheca Sacra,* vol. 72 (1915); *Neue Lutheranische Kirchenzeitung* (1895); A. J. Wilson, *Princeton Theological Review,* vol. 25 (1927).

Living Insights

This lesson gives us a wonderful overview of the Book of Jonah. Actually, the entire story is explained in forty-eight verses. Let's take a look at it paragraph by paragraph.

- The following chart divides the book into eleven paragraphs. Read each passage slowly and carefully. Next to the references on your chart, give each paragraph a title. It will take some thought, but have fun with this project. And by all means, be creative!

Overview of Jonah	
Paragraphs	Titles
1:1–3	
1:4–9	
1:10–14	
1:15–17	
2:1–9	
2:10	
3:1–4	
3:5–10	
4:1–4	
4:5–8	
4:9–11	

Living Insights

The greatest miracle in the Book of Jonah is not the incident with the "great fish." The greatest miracle is one of the most successful evangelistic crusades in the history of the world. Let's get a little closer to home. How does Jonah's life compare with yours?

- How open are you to sharing the gospel to the ends of the earth? Are there religious, cultural, or economic roadblocks that cause you to detour around certain people? How can you overcome this attitude and fulfill our Lord's great commission? Will you need a "great fish" to help you break through these barriers? As you ponder these questions, ask God to guide you to those who need to hear about Him. If you commit this to prayer now, you can avoid the whale's belly later!

The Prodigal Preacher

Jonah 1–2

Chapters 1 and 2 of Jonah show how God dealt with the disobedience of one of His messengers. Like a Wanted poster, these chapters depict Jonah as a fugitive. In a sermon on Jonah in the book *Moby Dick,* Father Mapple describes this runaway prophet.

"With this sin of disobedience in him, Jonah still further flouts at God, by seeking to flee from Him. He thinks that a ship made by men will carry him into countries where God does not reign, but only the Captains of this earth. He skulks about the wharves of Joppa, seeks a ship that's bound for Tarshish. . . . Miserable man! Oh! most contemptible and worthy of all scorn; with slouched hat and guilty eye, skulking from his God; prowling among the shipping like a vile burglar hastening to cross the seas. So disordered, self-condemning is his look, that had there been policemen in those days, Jonah, on the mere suspicion of something wrong, had been arrested ere he touched a deck. How plainly he's a fugitive! no baggage, not a hat-box, valise, or carpet-bag—no friends accompany him to the wharf with their adieux."[1]

Such is the sad, shadowy picture of a man going to great lengths to run from God. But as we shall see in this lesson, God will go to even greater lengths to retrieve him.

I. God's Command (Jonah 1:1–2)

The book begins in a dramatic and arresting way as God breaks the silence of heaven to give Jonah his missionary orders.

> The word of the Lord came to Jonah the son of Amittai saying, "Arise, go to Nineveh the great city, and cry against it, for their wickedness has come up before Me."

Traveling and preaching usually posed no problem to prophets. That was their job. But in this case, something churned Jonah's stomach—Nineveh. The very sound of it sickened him, because it was the capital of the vicious and godless Assyrians, Israel's archenemy. In every city they conquered, the Assyrians built a pyramid of human skulls. That was the brutal business card they left behind, and that was why Jonah responded as he did.

---

1. Herman Melville, *Moby Dick; or, The Whale,* in vol. 48 of *Great Books of the Western World,* ed. Robert Maynard Hutchins (Chicago, Ill.: Encyclopaedia Britannica, 1971), p. 31.

II. **Jonah's Disobedience** (Jonah 1:3)

From Jonah's perspective, God had gone too far. He was asking too much. So instead of arising . . . going . . . and crying out, Jonah arose . . . fled . . . and shipped out.[2]

> But Jonah rose up to flee to Tarshish from the presence of the Lord. So he went down to Joppa, found a ship which was going to Tarshish, paid the fare, and went down into it to go with them to Tarshish from the presence of the Lord.

The Futility of Fleeing

Are you, like Jonah, in the process of fleeing from the presence of God because He is asking you to do something that is just *too* much? Fleeing from the Lord is like trying to draw a round square. It's a logical impossibility. God is omnipresent—everywhere—and you can't escape from Someone who is everywhere.

> Where can I go from Thy Spirit?
> Or where can I flee from Thy presence?
> If I ascend to heaven, Thou art there;
> If I make my bed in Sheol, behold, Thou art there.
> If I take the wings of the dawn,
> If I dwell in the remotest part of the sea,
> Even there Thy hand will lead me,
> And Thy right hand will lay hold of me.
> If I say, "Surely the darkness will overwhelm me,
> And the light around me will be night,"
> Even the darkness is not dark to Thee,
> And the night is as bright as the day.
> Darkness and light are alike to Thee. (Ps. 139:7–12)

Whether you're on a raft in the middle of the ocean or in a cave in the cliffs of some mountain—He is there. Whether you are adrift in a sea of immorality or you have a heart that is hidden, distant, and cold—He is there.

III. **God's Response to Jonah's Disobedience** (Jonah 1:4–14)

God's plan to deliver Nineveh (see 2 Pet. 3:9) was not thwarted by a stubborn, strong-willed prophet, regardless of his credentials. God harnessed the wild winds of nature to hunt down this fugitive from faithfulness.

> And the Lord hurled a great wind on the sea and there was a great storm on the sea so that the ship was about to break up. (v. 4)

---

2. Tarshish was two thousand miles away from Nineveh and was the westernmost point on any trade route.

God's hunt for the prodigal prophet is tenaciously active. Notice the wording: "the Lord *hurled* a great wind" (emphasis added). God has his own way of bringing lost sheep back into His fold and will go to the ends of the earth and the depths of the oceans to do it. Apparently, the storm was so great that even the seasoned sailors on board feared for their lives and resorted to drastic measures.

> Then the sailors became afraid, and every man cried to his god, and they threw the cargo which was in the ship into the sea to lighten it for them. But Jonah had gone below into the hold of the ship, lain down, and fallen sound asleep. (v. 5)

It is said that there are no atheists at sea, and these sailors give evidence of that. Notice, however, where Jonah is. Safe below, sound asleep. But the frenzied captain soon changes all that.

> So the captain approached him and said, "How is it that you are sleeping? Get up, call on your god. Perhaps your god will be concerned about us so that we will not perish." And each man said to his mate, "Come, let us cast lots so we may learn on whose account this calamity has struck us." So they cast lots and the lot fell on Jonah. Then they said to him, "Tell us, now! On whose account has this calamity struck us? What is your occupation? And where do you come from? What is your country? From what people are you?" (vv. 6–8)

With the finger of accusation pointed at Jonah, the prophet reveals his identity and testifies.

> And he said to them, "I am a Hebrew, and I fear the Lord God of heaven who made the sea and the dry land." (v. 9)

Immediately, the sailors put this missing piece of information into the puzzle of the sudden storm.

> Then the men became extremely frightened and they said to him, "How could you do this?" For the men knew that he was fleeing from the presence of the Lord, because he had told them. (v. 10)

A Thought to Consider

When we're disobedient to God, our actions often have a negative effect, bringing a storm into our lives that can shipwreck the lives of those around us.

Desperately, the sailors plead with Jonah for a way to calm the storm.

> So they said to him, "What should we do to you that the sea may become calm for us?"—for the sea was becoming increasingly stormy. And he said to them, "Pick me

up and throw me into the sea. Then the sea will become calm for you, for I know that on account of me this great storm has come upon you." However, the men rowed desperately to return to land but they could not, for the sea was becoming even stormier against them. (vv. 11–13)

Hesitant to take a man's life, the sailors try to ride out the storm. Finally exhausting their human effort at the oars, the unbelieving sailors turn to God.

Then they called on the Lord and said, "We earnestly pray, O Lord, do not let us perish on account of this man's life and do not put innocent blood on us; for Thou, O Lord, hast done as Thou hast pleased." So they picked up Jonah, threw him into the sea, and the sea stopped its raging. (vv. 14–15)

The miraculous calming of the sea created an equally miraculous change in the lives of the sailors.

Then the men feared the Lord greatly, and they offered a sacrifice to the Lord and made vows. (v. 16)

IV. God's Salvation (Jonah 1:17)

God's salvation not only extends to the pagans in a spiritual sense, but goes even further to save the prophet in a physical sense. God does not abandon Jonah, regardless of his disobedience, but in an act of grace snatches him safely away.

And the Lord appointed a great fish to swallow Jonah, and Jonah was in the stomach of the fish three days and three nights.

Stomaching Difficult Circumstances

The brief description of Jonah's ordeal "in the stomach of the fish three days and three nights" is crisp and clean. But if you use your imagination to recreate the scene, it will terrify you. Pitch black. Sloshing gastric juices wash over you, burning skin, eyes, throat, nostrils. Oxygen is scarce and each frantic gulp of air is saturated with salt water. The rancid smell of digested food causes you to throw up repeatedly until you have only dry heaves left. Everything you touch has the slimy feel of the mucous membrane that lines the stomach. You feel claustrophobic. With every turn and dive of the great fish, you slip and slide in the cesspool of digestive fluid. There are no footholds. No blankets to keep you warm from the cold, clammy depths of the sea. For three days and three nights you endure this harsh womb of God's grace. His grace sometimes comes to us in ways we would never expect. Does God have you in the stomach of some dark, slippery, distasteful circumstances?

> If so, prayer is the only lamp by which you will see beyond the darkness and through to the Savior's grace.

V. Jonah's Prayer (Jonah 2:1–10)

From the murky depths of despair, Jonah calls out to God for deliverance.

> Then Jonah prayed to the Lord his God from the stomach
> of the fish, and he said,
> "I called out of my distress to the Lord,
> And He answered me.
> I cried for help from the depth of Sheol;
> Thou didst hear my voice.
> For Thou hadst cast me into the deep,
> Into the heart of the seas,
> And the current engulfed me.
> All Thy breakers and billows passed over me.
> So I said, 'I have been expelled from Thy sight.
> Nevertheless I will look again toward Thy holy temple.'
> Water encompassed me to the point of death.
> The great deep engulfed me,
> Weeds were wrapped around my head.
> I descended to the roots of the mountains.
> The earth with its bars was around me forever,
> But Thou hast brought up my life from the pit, O Lord
> my God.
> While I was fainting away,
> I remembered the Lord;
> And my prayer came to Thee,
> Into Thy holy temple.
> Those who regard vain idols
> Forsake their faithfulness,
> But I will sacrifice to Thee
> With the voice of thanksgiving.
> That which I have vowed I will pay.
> Salvation is from the Lord."
> Then the Lord commanded the fish, and it vomited Jonah
> up onto the dry land.

Jonah cries out in verse 3: "For Thou hast cast me into the deep." But who threw him overboard? The sailors, right? Yes, but ultimately Jonah sees God behind his circumstances. That's looking at life from God's point of view. That's insightful perspective and wisdom. Perspective like that in the face of trials comes only through the light of prayer. In the context of trials, James writes: "But if any of you lacks wisdom, let him ask of God, who gives to all men generously and without reproach, and it will be given to him" (1:5). Sometimes it's difficult to see God's hand stirring the storm. There are times when we are thrown overboard and fail to recognize that He is doing the tossing. There are times, too, when we are swallowed by monstrous circumstances and held captive (Jon. 2:6), and fail to understand that the great fish was "appointed" by God. Prayer is what gives us three-dimensional perspective to see God at work in our lives. If the prayer in Jonah 2 teaches us anything, it instructs us that we can pray anytime, anywhere, and have confidence that no matter how suffocating and slimy our circumstances, our prayers will come before the Lord God of heaven in His holy temple (v. 7).

Living Insights

Study One

In our last lesson, we studied the Book of Jonah by looking at each paragraph individually. Let's shift our focus to a biographical sketch of this prophet.

- Based on your understanding of the Book of Jonah, try your hand at writing a character study of the *man* Jonah. The best way to do this is to reread the book, making notes along the way of significant demonstrations of Jonah's character. Then, gather your notes and rewrite them in a creative way. Perhaps you could write a letter of recommendation on Jonah's behalf. Maybe you'd like to write an article for a newspaper or magazine. Be as creative and imaginative as the text will allow. It will help you see this man as he really was.

Living Insights

Study Two

After an exercise like the previous character study, the next step is to compare and contrast yourself to Jonah. How do you look alongside this famous biblical character?

- Make a copy of the following chart in your notebook. Refer back to your notes from the previous Living Insights and ask yourself the following questions: In what ways are Jonah and I *alike?* In what ways are we *different?* Write your answers in the appropriate columns.

Jonah and I	
Similarities	Differences

Revival! In Spite of the Evangelist
Jonah 3–4

The greatest revival in the history of the world took place in a very unlikely spot on the globe. It did not occur in Scotland, as a result of John Knox's influence. Nor did it take place in England, connected with Wesley, Spurgeon, G. Campbell Morgan, or F. B. Meyer. It was not in Europe, in spite of the impact of Calvin, Luther, Zwingli, or Savonarola. Neither was it in America, although we have been blessed with the ministries of Moody, Gypsy Smith, Jonathan Edwards, Billy Sunday, and Billy Graham. Give up? It occurred 150 miles northwest of Baghdad, near the modern city of Mosul.[1] In the vicinity of Mosul is a massive mound of earth. Beneath that mound, we are told, is the ancient tomb of the evangelist responsible for this great revival—the prophet Jonah.[2] When we think of Jonah, we think of resistance . . . rebellion . . . retreat. But what *should* stand out in our thinking is revival, for through his preaching the entire city of Nineveh experienced a dramatic conversion. So far, we have seen Jonah running *from* God in chapter 1 and *to* God in chapter 2. As our study opens in chapter 3, we see him running *with* God in obedience.

I. Jonah's Revival (Jonah 3:1–4)

After walking out on the job, Jonah returns to God with a repentant heart and is given a second chance. He embarks on the single greatest missionary effort of all time. Physically, the journey was difficult. Jonah's trek from the eastern shore of the Mediterranean to Nineveh spanned approximately five hundred miles. Politically, making the journey worse, he was traveling in enemy territory. Spiritually, the assignment was undoubtedly hard for Jonah, as he was given no latitude with regard to his message. God instructed him: "Proclaim to it the proclamation which I am going to tell you" (v. 2b).[3] In verse 3, Nineveh is described as "an exceedingly great city, a three days' walk." As Californians designate Los Angeles to incorporate many smaller cities and suburbs, so the Hebrews designated several cities within the Nineveh metropolis.

> From that land he went forth into Assyria, and built Nineveh and Rehoboth-Ir and Calah, and Resen between Nineveh and Calah; that is the great city. (Gen. 10:11–12)

---

1. Merrill F. Unger, *Archaeology and the Old Testament* (Grand Rapids, Mich.: Zondervan Publishing House, 1970), p. 263.

2. The mound is named Nebi Yunus, Hebrew for "Prophet Jonah."

3. In Hebrew the "I" is the most emphatic word in the sentence. The sense of the sentence is: "*I* will give you the message to proclaim."

Therefore, a three days' walk through the city would be entirely reasonable.[4] During the first monotonous day of his walk, Jonah trudges the streets of this foreign metropolis—one small man calling out like a town crier against this sprawling Sodom of a city. Like a broken record, he parrots the same song: "Yet forty days and Nineveh will be overthrown . . . Yet forty days and Nineveh will be overthrown . . . Yet forty days and Nineveh will be overthrown."

God of the Second Chance

The statement, "Now the word of the Lord came to Jonah the *second* time" (Jon. 3:1, emphasis added), reveals a great deal about God's character. He doesn't turn a deaf ear or a cold shoulder to the repentant—no matter how blatant the rebellion or which borders the runaway crosses. Like the father in the story of the Prodigal Son, God waits with open arms, fatted calf, robe, and ring to give us a second chance to serve Him.

II. Nineveh's Repentance (Jonah 3:5–10)

Illustrating Hebrews 4:12, the living and active Word of God cuts like a sharp, two-edged sword to pierce the hearts of the Ninevites.

Then the people of Nineveh believed in God; and they called a fast and put on sackcloth from the greatest to the least of them. When the word reached the king of Nineveh, he arose from his throne, laid aside his robe from him, covered himself with sackcloth, and sat on the ashes. And he issued a proclamation and it said, "In Nineveh by the decree of the king and his nobles: Do not let man, beast, herd, or flock taste a thing. Do not let them eat or drink water. But both man and beast must be covered with sackcloth; and let men call on God earnestly that each may turn from his wicked way and from the violence which is in his hands. Who knows, God may turn and relent, and withdraw His burning anger so that we shall not perish?" When God saw their deeds, that they turned from their wicked way, then God relented concerning the calamity which He had declared He would bring upon them. And He did not do it.

Even the king of Nineveh, sitting in his palace, is touched by the carefully honed point of Jonah's message. At once, he abdicates his

---

4. If Herodotus's definition of a day's march as seventeen days is used, then the great city's diameter was approximately fifty miles. Leslie C. Allen, *The Books of Joel, Obadiah, Jonah, and Micah,* in *International Commentary on the Old Testament* (Grand Rapids, Mich.: William B. Eerdmans Publishing Co., 1976), p. 221.

high position in the ominous face of God's wrath. "His *throne* and *royal robes* are exchanged for *sackcloth* and *ashes*."[5] The repentance extends from "the greatest to the least"—from king to commoner, from man to beast.[6]

"Yet even now," declares the Lord,
"Return to Me with all your heart,
And with fasting, weeping, and mourning;
And rend your heart and not your garments."
Now return to the Lord your God,
For He is gracious and compassionate,
Slow to anger, abounding in lovingkindness,
And relenting of evil. (Joel 2:12–13)

III. Jonah's Reaction (Jonah 4:1–4)

The heat of God's anger is cooled by the tears of Nineveh's repentance. In His mercy He issues a death-row reprieve from their slated execution. Jonah's reaction, however, is totally opposite. Instead of reacting like the Prodigal Son's compassionate father, Jonah responds in a way that parallels the critical older brother (Luke 15:28).

> But it greatly displeased Jonah, and he became angry. And he prayed to the Lord and said, "Please Lord, was not this what I said while I was still in my own country? Therefore, in order to forestall this I fled to Tarshish, for I knew that Thou art a gracious and compassionate God, slow to anger and abundant in lovingkindness, and one who relents concerning calamity. Therefore now, O Lord, please take my life from me, for death is better to me than life." And the Lord said, "Do you have good reason to be angry?"

Notice carefully how God deals with the pouting prophet. No sermon. No rebuke. No argument. Just the barbed question that hung like a fishhook in his heart: "Do you have good reason to be angry?"

Classroom Theology/Calloused Heart

It is possible to have all the right theology while having a totally wrong heart. Notice how accurate, how biblical Jonah's theology is: "I knew that Thou art a gracious and compassionate God, slow to anger and abundant in lovingkindness, and one who relents concerning calamity" (v. 2b). Notice also his anger (v. 1). Right words, wrong heart. The parables in Luke 15

---

5. Allen, *Joel, Obadiah, Jonah, and Micah,* p. 224.

6. "It was a Persian custom for animals to participate in mourning ceremonies. . . . The gesture would impress forcibly . . . the sincerity of Nineveh's repentance." Allen, *Joel, Obadiah, Jonah, and Micah,* p. 224.

picture how our hearts should respond when a sinner repents. In each incident—the lost sheep (vv. 3–7), the lost coin (vv. 8–10), the lost son (vv. 11–32)—what was lost was found, resulting in great joy (vv. 7, 10, and 32). Climactically, the father in the parable of the Prodigal Son illustrates the embracing, compassionate heart of God the Father toward a wayward child. In contrast, the critical older brother illustrates the indignant, self-righteous heart of the Pharisees and scribes (v. 2). Two portraits. A compassionate, accepting father. A critical, angry brother. You can dot every theological *i* and cross every exegetical *t*, but still be a great distance from God. As Jesus said to the hypocrites:

> " 'This people honors Me with their lips,
> But their heart is far away from Me.' " (Mark 7:6b)

The Prodigal Son's brother lived under the same roof as the father, but his heart was miles away. How about you? How close is your heart to the Father's?

IV. God's Rebuke (Jonah 4:5–11)

Stomping off in a huff, Jonah shook the city's dust off his feet and built a box seat on a hillside to view the city's fate.

> Then Jonah went out from the city and sat east of it. There he made a shelter for himself and sat under it in the shade until he could see what would happen in the city. (v. 5)

The God of the sea, who can appoint a great fish to swallow Jonah, is also the God of the earth, who can appoint a plant to shade him.

> So the Lord God appointed a plant and it grew up over Jonah to be a shade over his head to deliver him from his discomfort. And Jonah was extremely happy about the plant. (v. 6)

Note the great emotional response that this lower level of life brought to Jonah: "And Jonah was extremely happy about the plant." With this plant, God sows an object lesson in the hard soil of Jonah's heart.

> But God appointed a worm when dawn came the next day, and it attacked the plant and it withered. And it came about when the sun came up that God appointed a scorching east wind, and the sun beat down on Jonah's head so that he became faint and begged with all his soul to die, saying, "Death is better to me than life." (vv. 7–8)

God again appoints another of his creatures—this time a worm, and this time for destruction. Not only is Jonah's shade gone, but God appoints a scorching east wind. As the sun beats down on Jonah, his joy shrivels like the leaves of the plant. Longing for death, Jonah calls out to God in despair. But there is no salve from God; only the same type of stinging question that sought him before.

> Then God said to Jonah, "Do you have good reason to be angry about the plant?" And he said, "I have good reason to be angry, even to death." (v. 9)

Jonah's answer forms a fist in God's face, but fails to ruffle the calm feathers of His patient instruction.

> Then the Lord said, "You had compassion on the plant for which you did not work, and which you did not cause to grow, which came up overnight and perished overnight. And should I not have compassion on Nineveh, the great city in which there are more than 120,000 persons who do not know the difference between their right and left hand, as well as many animals?" (vv. 10–11)

God's words pour into Jonah's soul like salt into sun-scorched blisters. With a light hand but a sharp hoe, God cultivates the object lesson He planted in Jonah's heart. Essentially, God puts His arm around Jonah and seems to be saying, "Let's talk about this concern you had for the plant, Jonah."

> "What did it really mean to you? Your attachment to it could not be very deep, for it was here one day and *gone the next.* Your concern was dictated by self-interest, not by a genuine love. You never had for it the devotion of the gardener. If you feel as badly as you do, what would you expect a gardener to feel like, who tended a plant and watched it grow only to see it wither and die, poor thing? And this is how I feel about Nineveh, only much more so. All those people, all those animals—I made them, I have cherished them all these years. Nineveh has cost me no end of effort, and they mean the world to me. Your pain is nothing to mine when I contemplate their destruction."[7]

With the object lesson deeply rooted in Jonah's heart, the embittered prophet stands silent before the court of heaven—a mute testimony to the truth of God's argument. And thus we leave Jonah—never to hear his voice in the Scriptures again.

The Lesson of Jonah

Jonah's value scale was so unbalanced . . . his vision, so nearsighted . . . his life, so small. An insignificant, soulless plant meant more to him than anything on earth. The lesson of the

7. Allen, *Joel, Obadiah, Jonah, and Micah,* p. 234.

book is that Jonah was more concerned about Jonah than he was about Nineveh. What's the lesson of your life? Are you more concerned with building shelters and raising plants—more concerned about creature comforts and selfish living—than the deep, spiritual needs of people? Are there some plants in your life that need to be removed so you can see your Nineveh?

Living Insights

Study One

Have you found this study of Old Testament characters stimulating? We've looked at both the well-known and the relatively unknown. Most likely, some truths stood out above the others. Let's look at a few.

- Flip back through your notebook and study guide, and pick out one significant *truth* from each lesson. Jot it down on a copy of the following chart. Zero in on truths; we will address application in study two.

Old Testament Characters	
Titles	Truths
Samson: A He-Man with a She-Weakness	
Samson: How the Mighty Are Fallen!	
Abigail: A Woman of Wisdom	
Absalom: The Rebel Prince Charming	
Rehoboam: The Reckless Phony	
Naaman and Gehazi: Characters in Contrast	
Jabez: Disabled but Not Disqualified	
Uzziah: The King Who Became a Leper	
From Captive to Queen: An Adoption Story	
Mr. Jones, Meet Mr. Jonah	
The Prodigal Preacher	
Revival! In Spite of the Evangelist	

Continued on next page

Living Insights

No review of these character studies would be complete without a look at the changes in our lives that result. Living Insights are designed with application in mind. Let's look back over the most meaningful ones we learned.

- The following chart is identical to the one in study one, but now we are looking for *application*. Look through your study guide and notebook; pick one meaningful application from each lesson.

Old Testament Characters	
Titles	Applications
Samson: A He-Man with a She-Weakness	
Samson: How the Mighty Are Fallen!	
Abigail: A Woman of Wisdom	
Absalom: The Rebel Prince Charming	
Rehoboam: The Reckless Phony	
Naaman and Gehazi: Characters in Contrast	
Jabez: Disabled but Not Disqualified	
Uzziah: The King Who Became a Leper	
From Captive to Queen: An Adoption Story	
Mr. Jones, Meet Mr. Jonah	
The Prodigal Preacher	
Revival! In Spite of the Evangelist	

Books for Probing Further

In his essay *Reflections in Westminster Abbey,* seventeenth-century writer Joseph Addison records his thoughts on a stroll through the famed British cemetery:

> When I look upon the tombs of the great, every emotion of envy dies in me. When I read the epitaphs of the beautiful, every inordinate desire goes out. When I meet with the grief of parents upon a tombstone, my heart melts with compassion. When I see the tomb of the parents themselves, I consider the vanity of grieving for those whom we must quickly follow. When I see kings lying by those who deposed them, when I consider rival wits placed side by side, or the holy men that divided the world with their contests and disputes, I reflect with sorrow and astonishment on the little competitions, factions, and debates of mankind. When I read the several dates of the tombs, of some that died yesterday, and some six hundred years ago, I consider that great day when we shall all of us be contemporaries, and make our appearance together.[1]

Death is the common denominator of all mankind. And epitaphs, like file folder tabs, serve to summarize our lives in the fewest words possible. The titles to our studies on *Old Testament Characters* have summarily reduced their lives, like epitaphs, for convenient mental reference.

"Samson: How the Mighty Are Fallen!"
"Abigail: A Woman of Wisdom"
"Absalom: The Rebel Prince Charming"
"Rehoboam: The Reckless Phony"
"Naaman and Gehazi: Characters in Contrast"
"Jabez: Disabled but Not Disqualified"
"Uzziah: The King Who Became a Leper"
"Esther: From Captive to Queen"
"Jonah: The Prodigal Preacher"

When we think of specific biblical characters, certain associations come immediately to mind. For example, what association do you make when you think of the Apostle John? Probably the words "the disciple whom Jesus loved" pop into your mind. How about when you think about Judas? Does the word *traitor* burn before your eyes? Or Peter? Mary and Martha? The rich young ruler? The Prodigal Son? The word or words that come immediately to mind form the premise of that person's life ... what that person stood for ... what that person's life meant. What words or phrases come to mind when people think of your life? What images flash on their mental screens?

1. *The Original McGuffey's: The Fourth Eclectic Reader,* ed. Jean Morton (Milford, Mich.: Mott Media, 1982), pp. 401–2.

I hope you have benefited from our brief walk through the cemetery where the Old Testament characters are buried. There's nothing like the cold granite reality that death forces us to touch—the reality that one day, each of us will be there too. Each with a tombstone. Each with an epitaph etched in eternity.

The tombstones of most of our Old Testament characters are splotched with sin. Lust, greed, pride, ambition, deception, bitterness, and rebellion crawl over the headstones like lichen. Listed below are several books that I think will substantially help polish the marble of your life and help set your life on the solid premise of God's Word, His love, and eternity.

Petersen, J. Allen. *The Myth of the Greener Grass.* Wheaton, Ill.: Tyndale House Publishers, 1983. Like Delilah enticing Samson, the flame of adultery may first appear warm and comforting, but in the final analysis, it sears and scars its participants. Many a marriage has been reduced to ashes because of infidelity. Is there hope for a relationship charred by adultery? Can there be forgiveness? Can oneness be restored? The author deals with these difficult questions in the light of both modern psychology and the truth of God's Word. With sensitivity and insight he unearths the root causes of the problem, warning signs of a deteriorating marriage, and ways to "affair-proof" a healthy marriage.

Schaeffer, Edith. *A Way of Seeing.* Old Tappan, N.J.: Fleming H. Revell Co., 1977. One of the reasons some of the Old Testament characters got into trouble on such a catastrophic scale was the presence of blind spots. If they had developed a different way of seeing—more sensitive, more responsive—much pain could have been averted. *A Way of Seeing* will open up a new way of looking at life in general, and at *your* life in particular. In this personal kaleidoscope the author gives us vivid glimpses of daily life, illuminating such concepts as trust, faith, security, death, love, and fear. These pieces were first written for the magazine *Christianity Today* and later compiled into a book due to enthusiastic reader response.

Swindoll, Charles R. *Strike the Original Match.* Portland, Oreg.: Multnomah Press, 1980. Abigail was an example of a woman who tried faithfully to hold her marriage together. No easy task, for building a good marriage is a lot like building a fine home. The architect must be consulted, a solid foundation poured, and the best material used. And, no matter how fine a finished product, termites can always destroy it. Recognizing that the idea of marriage originated with God, this book calls for a fresh and detailed look at His original blueprint and offers practical, positive advice.

White, John. *Eros Defiled: The Christian and Sexual Sin.* Downers Grove, Ill.: InterVarsity Press, 1978. In spite of Samson's strength, he succumbed to one weakness—lust. Similarly, sexual sin has destroyed many a strong person, strong marriage, strong family, strong church. With a Christlike mixture of compassion and conviction—"grace and truth"—Dr. White speaks openly about the Christian and sexual sin.

———. *The Fight.* Downers Grove, Ill.: InterVarsity Press, 1978. The epitaphs of our Old Testament characters, by and large, look like a graveyard of defeated people. Rehoboam was defeated by ambition, Gehazi by greed, Uzziah by pride. Only a few—Abigail, Naaman, Jabez—triumphed in their faith. The life of faith is a constant struggle with "the world, the flesh, and the devil." There *is* joy and triumph in the Christian life, but it is often preceded by and mysteriously intertwined with struggle. White takes us through the basic areas of Christian living that we wrestle with throughout our lives: faith, prayer, temptation, evangelism, guidance, Bible study, fellowship, work. Applied, this book can help build a warmly remembered epitaph that will stand the tests of both time and eternity.

———. *Parents in Pain.* Downers Grove, Ill.: InterVarsity Press, 1979. Parental pain is almost universal to one degree or another. Even Israel's greatest king, David, experienced great pain with his son Absalom. Undoubtedly, many parents cannot cope with the problems they must face with their children—rebellion, runaways, substance abuse, homosexuality, even suicide. In this unique book, the author doesn't give pat prescriptions to straighten out your child. Rather, he helps *you,* as a parent, deal with your sense of guilt, frustration, anger, and inadequacy.

Acknowledgments

Insight for Living is grateful for permission to quote from the following source:

Carmichael, Amy. *Toward Jerusalem.* Fort Washington, Pa.: Christian Literature Crusade, 1961; London, England: Society for Promoting Christian Knowledge, 1950.

Insight for Living
Cassette Tapes
OLD TESTAMENT CHARACTERS

Scriptural character studies never fail to encourage us in our pilgrimage. That is one of the reasons God included snapshots of so many people in His Book. He wants us to see His truth reflected in all these lives—even in the most obscure and unfamiliar individuals.

These messages will introduce ten Old Testament personalities to you. As they are unveiled, the end goal is that you will receive helpful perspective and wisdom that will result in greater stability, a stronger commitment to biblical principles, and a broader awareness of how God works in our lives today.

			U.S.	Canadian
OTC	CS	Cassette series—includes album cover	$34.50	$43.75
		Individual cassettes—include messages		
		A and B	5.00	6.35

These prices are effective as of November 1986 and are subject to change without notice.

OTC **1-A:** *Samson: A He-Man with a She-Weakness*—Judges 13–15
      B: *Samson: How the Mighty Are Fallen!*—Judges 16:4–31

OTC **2-A:** *Abigail: A Woman of Wisdom*—1 Samuel 25
      B: *Absalom: The Rebel Prince Charming*—2 Samuel 13–18

OTC **3-A:** *Rehoboam: The Reckless Phony*—1 Kings 11–14
      B: *Naaman and Gehazi: Characters in Contrast*—2 Kings 5

OTC **4-A:** *Jabez: Disabled but Not Disqualified*—1 Chronicles 4:9–10
      B: *Uzziah: The King Who Became a Leper*—2 Chronicles 26

OTC **5-A:** *From Captive to Queen: An Adoption Story*—Romans 8,
      Galatians 4, Esther
      B: *Mr. Jones, Meet Mr. Jonah*—Jonah

OTC **6-A:** *The Prodigal Preacher*—Jonah 1–2
      B: *Revival! In Spite of the Evangelist*—Jonah 3–4

Ordering Information

U.S. ordering information: You are welcome to use our toll-free number (for Visa and MasterCard orders only) between the hours of 8:30 A.M. and 4:00 P.M., Pacific time, Monday through Friday. The number is **(800) 772-8888.** This number may be used anywhere in the continental United States excluding California, Hawaii, and Alaska. Orders from those areas are handled through our Sales Department at **(714) 870-9161.** We are unable to accept collect calls.

Your order will be processed promptly. We ask that you allow four to six weeks for delivery by fourth-class mail. If you wish your order to be shipped first-class, please add 10 percent of the total order cost (not including California sales tax) for shipping and handling.

Canadian ordering information: Your order will be processed promptly. We ask that you allow approximately four weeks for delivery by first-class mail to the U.S./Canadian border. All orders will be shipped from our office in Fullerton, California. For our listeners in British Columbia, a 7 percent sales tax must be added to the total of all tape orders (not including first-class postage). For further information, please contact our office at **(604) 272-5811.**

Payment options: We accept personal checks, money orders, Visa, and MasterCard in payment for materials ordered. Unfortunately, we are unable to offer invoicing or COD orders. If the amount of your check or money order is less than the amount of your purchase, your check will be returned so that you may place your order again with the correct amount. All orders must be paid in full before shipment can be made.

Returned checks: There is a $10 charge for any returned check (regardless of the amount of your order) to cover processing and invoicing.

Guarantee: Our tapes are guaranteed for ninety days against faulty performance or breakage due to a defect in the tape. For best results, please be sure your tape recorder is in good operating condition and is cleaned regularly.

Mail your order to one of the following addresses:

Insight for Living
Sales Department
Post Office Box 4444
Fullerton, CA 92634

Insight for Living Ministries
Post Office Box 2510
Vancouver, BC
Canada V6B 3W7

Quantity discounts and gift certificates are available upon request.

Overseas ordering information is provided on the reverse side of the order form.

Order Form

Please send me the following cassette tapes:

The current series: ☐ OTC CS Old Testament Characters
Individual cassettes: ☐ OTC 1 ☐ OTC 2 ☐ OTC 3
☐ OTC 4 ☐ OTC 5 ☐ OTC 6

I am enclosing:

$ _____ To purchase the cassette series for $34.50 (in Canada $43.75*) which includes the album cover

$ _____ To purchase individual tapes at $5.00 each (in Canada $6.35*)

$ _____ Total of purchases

$ _____ If the order will be delivered in California, please add 6 percent sales tax

$ _____ U.S. residents please add 10 percent for first-class shipping and handling if desired

$ _____ *British Columbia residents please add 7 percent sales tax

$ _____ Canadian residents please add 6 percent for postage

$ _____ **Overseas residents please add appropriate postage** (See postage chart under "Overseas Ordering Information.")

$ _____ As a gift to the Insight for Living radio ministry for which a tax-deductible receipt will be issued

$ _____ **Total amount due (Please do not send cash.)**

Form of payment:

☐ Check or money order made payable to Insight for Living
☐ Credit card (Visa or MasterCard only)
If there is a balance: ☐ apply it as a donation ☐ please refund

---

Credit card purchases:
☐ Visa ☐ MasterCard number _____
Expiration date _____
Signature _____
We cannot process your credit card purchase without your signature.

Name _____

Address _____

_____

City _____

State/Province _____ Zip/Postal code _____

Country _____

Telephone ( ) _____ Radio station ___ ___ ___ ___

Should questions arise concerning your order, we may need to contact you.

Overseas Ordering Information

If you do not live in the United States or Canada, please note the following information. This will ensure efficient processing of your request.

Estimated time of delivery: We ask that you allow approximately twelve to sixteen weeks for delivery by surface mail. If you would like your order sent airmail, the length of delivery may be reduced. All orders will be shipped from our office in Fullerton, California.

Payment options: Due to fluctuating currency rates, we can accept only personal checks made payable in U.S. funds, international money orders, Visa, and MasterCard in payment for materials ordered. If the amount of your check or money order is less than the amount of your purchase, your check will be returned so that you may place your order again with the correct amount. All orders must be paid in full before shipment can be made.

Returned checks: There is a $10 charge for any returned check (regardless of the amount of your order) to cover processing and invoicing.

Postage and handling: Please add to the amount of purchase the postage cost for the service you desire. All orders must include postage based on the chart below.

Purchase Amount		Surface Postage	Airmail Postage
From	To	Percentage of Order	Percentage of Order
$ .01	$15.00	40%	75%
15.01	75.00	25%	45%
75.01	or more	15%	40%

Guarantee: Our tapes are guaranteed for ninety days against faulty performance or breakage due to a defect in the tape. For best results, please be sure your tape recorder is in good operating condition and is cleaned regularly.

Mail your order or inquiry to the following address:

Insight for Living
Sales Department
Post Office Box 4444
Fullerton, CA 92634

Quantity discounts and gift certificates are available upon request.